LEASH *of* COURAGE

ONE WHISTLEBLOWER'S CRUSADE AGAINST BIG PHARMA
FRAUD AND HER GOLDEN PATH TO HEALING

NOELLE WEBB

Leash of Courage: One Whistleblower's Crusade Against Big Pharma Fraud and Her Golden Path to Healing

Copyright © Noelle Webb (2026)

ISBN Paperback: 979-8-89576-183-0
ISBN Hardback: 979-8-89576-184-7

Published by:

To all the brave and beautiful souls, human and canine, who feel discarded, abandoned, and alone. I hope this story brings healing to your heart and courage to your crusade.

Table of Contents

Introduction

*"I no longer feared the darkness once I knew
the phoenix in me would rise from the ashes."*
—William C. Hannan

Imagine a sunny summer day in the small front yard of a modest brick home. A young girl is laughing and running in circles on the freshly cut grass while a black puppy nips playfully at her flip-flops. Her father sits on the small brick stoop at the front door, smiling at the young girl and puppy playing their game of chase. The child squeals with delight.

It sounds idyllic, doesn't it? It was. This is my very first memory. I remember the colors: the vividly bright blue sky, the vibrant green grass, and the intense jet black of my dog's fur. My pink flip-flops were laced with tiny puppy tooth marks. When I close my eyes, I am transported back in time to that iconic moment of happiness and safety.

The elements of that memory still bring me comfort today: a warm, sunny summer day, bright blue skies, the smell of freshly cut grass, but more significantly, the joy of being with my dad and my dog. The power of that simple memory is breathtaking, especially now because my father, my childhood dog, and time have passed away. But I still smile when the recollection drifts through my consciousness.

Over the last decade, my life has unexpectedly changed. That tiny girl grew up to become a whistleblower.

Today, I find myself on the quasi-winning side of 11 years of protracted litigation. I had the courage to take a stand against fraud in corporate America when no one else would. I was knocked down, trampled upon, financially devastated, and left to live out an unremarkable life.

But I would not and will not "go gently into that good night."

Where did my courage, strength, and perseverance come from? What motivated me to begin again and rebuild a purpose-filled life? The answer lies in my earliest memory. The courage came from my father, and the motivation to re-engage with life was a gift from my dog.

This book is about my journey of whistleblowing, retaliation, and resilience as my life came full circle. I am sharing my story in the hope that it will inspire you, ignite the fire in your soul, and give you the strength and courage to face whatever obstacles life places in your path. Above all, I want you to believe in your ability to rise like a phoenix from your own ashes to become brighter and more beautiful than ever before.

CHAPTER 1

The Code

"Truth has no special time of its own.
Its hour is now—always."
—Albert Schweitzer

The rendezvous location was only 10 minutes from my house. I wanted to stay local in case I was kidnapped and blindfolded because I could probably figure out my holding location due to 30 years of familiarity with my community. My vision is my kryptonite, so for many years I had visualized routes in my brain, even to the point of counting steps between rooms in my house as I prepared myself for future vision loss. We had agreed on a busy Panera restaurant at high noon. I had never met the person to whom I would be handing off sensitive, incriminating documents, so I needed as many eyes on the "drop" as possible, just in case it all went south.

I'd read the books about whistleblowers: nothing good ever happened to them, so I felt the weight of what I was about to do. In my mind, kidnapping and murder were definite possibilities. It would probably go down within minutes of my arrival at our agreed-upon rendezvous location.

After my tumultuous resignation from Depomed in 2013, I'd been searching for a lawyer to take up my pharmaceutical fraud whistleblower case. I'd met with several different lawyers, but they didn't seem to grasp the illegalities I was laying out. What I did not know at the time was that *qui tam* False Claims Act litigation is quite specialized and requires a lawyer experienced in that type of case. I hit roadblock after roadblock on the lawyer front, and I was about to admit defeat, chalking the experience up to one more unethical, greedy pharmaceutical company and a poor choice of employers on my part, and then something unexpected happened.

A year after my resignation from Depomed, I was diligently looking for another job and getting nowhere. Discouraged and running low on money and confidence, I broadened my search to anything else for which I might be qualified or, more likely, over-qualified. My expectations of finding something within the pharma industry were diminishing, and I began to consider the possibility that Depomed HR may have altered my employment status to "fired" rather than "resigned." I had no evidence of this other than the fact that I was perfectly qualified and quickly rejected for the jobs I was applying for. I would occasionally get an interview and advance through nearly the entire hiring process only to be abruptly told, "Sorry, we have decided to move forward with someone else." No explanation was ever offered, even when I requested it. Human resources personnel are well-trained in vagueness and avoiding any type of explanation that could possibly lead to litigation. This scenario, though, played out often enough that my gut-checker was on high alert.

After my routine morning coffee with my husband, I'd sit down at my desk looking for any new or unusual job postings online. One morning, I ran across a posting that looked like it had been written with me in mind.

Fraud Consultant—Specialty Pharma/Device/Oncology/Cardiology/Home Health—Richmond

I couldn't believe what I was reading. "Do you think this is legit?" I asked my husband. My radar sensed it might be too good to be true, but he was not convinced it was suspicious and suggested I answer it. And so I did. I was intrigued and desperate enough to send in my résumé.

In less than 24 hours, I received a call from a personable young man who wanted to know about my experience, and if I had ever witnessed fraud in the pharmaceutical industry. Well, yes, of course I had—anyone who has spent more than a month in that industry has witnessed fraud. But what made me different was that I was willing to share what I had seen and heard. The screener was more than a little impressed, and I'm sure I came off as more than a little eager.

We spoke for about 30 minutes, and as we wrapped up the call, he said, "We're very interested in your information. Someone will be calling you."

It was a very odd way for a job screener to politely end a normal conversation. The words he used and his definite tone of voice were not the standard HR tone I had grown accustomed to over my past year of job hunting. The possibility of finding and confronting fraud in the pharma industry appealed to me because I knew exactly what it looked like. I was an insider, so to speak, so I knew I could convince others in the industry to open up to me. I was made for this opportunity; now I just had to convince the next person I spoke to that this was most definitely in my wheelhouse.

Quite unexpectedly, the next interview with a pleasantly upbeat lawyer took place within 24 hours. He explained that his company was very interested in the information I had gathered on Depomed.

Wait. What?

I'd thought I was applying for a job as a fraud examiner, but this did not sound like a job interview at all. His explanation of the discrepancy was rather slippery and vague, as he quickly steered the conversation to my documents. I had been duped. Unfortunately, it would not be the only time in this decades-long saga.

The sting of being so gullible was offset by the possibility that an actual whistleblower lawyer would review my documents and let me know if my case was valid or just pie-in-the-sky. We agreed on a date, time, and place to meet. The legal phase of my unexpected journey was about to begin.

On the morning of the meeting, I copied and stashed my incriminating documents, in chronological order, in a plain 9 ×

12 manila envelope, while preserving the originals in a locked file cabinet at home. The envelope had to be nondescript because that's how all secretive information is passed from one person to another—at least that's how it's done in spy films. And while this was not a 007 movie, it was probably as close as anything else would be in my fairly normal life. But I had questions. I'd already been fooled into believing this was a job interview. What if I was being played again? Who was this person I was supposed to meet? Yes, I had googled him, but what if he was lying? What if this was all a setup? What if they took my information and I never saw them again? What if this were a mole from Depomed and they were going through back channels to figure out what evidence I had? The entire scenario felt a bit James Bond-like, and I began to think I might not be a very good candidate for spydom.

To say I was nervous is like saying Virginia is pleasantly warm in the summertime. My beautiful home state is like the depths of hell in July, with its high heat and even higher humidity. But mid-July was the planned meeting date with Mr. Unknown Lawyer. To make matters worse, I'd recently been in a bicycle accident and was still feeling the effects of a fractured pelvis and a torn rotator cuff. Recent shoulder surgery had left me wearing a bulky cast to keep my right shoulder immobilized. Being right-handed, I was physically vulnerable, and the uncertainty of the upcoming meeting left me feeling exposed and emotionally vulnerable.

Because I had developed a generous amount of resilience over my lifetime, I accepted the challenge of approaching life left-handed. Albeit a temporary situation, I thought it might be an interesting new skill to develop. I learned to eat, write, bathe, and prepare meals as a leftie, but there was one task that was literally out of my reach—managing my thick, long, curly hair. As the meeting date approached, I became unduly worried, not only about my upcoming kidnapping, but also about my wild and unruly hair! As a sales executive, I'd spent decades playing the role of the polished, confident professional. While I was aware of the absurdity of my feelings, it was not a role I could easily erase from my persona. Oddly enough, it never occurred to me that if I were going to be kidnapped, my hair would be the least of my concerns.

In a moment of desperation, I asked my husband to help me with my hair, which was probably worse than doing it myself with my left hand. Hair discussion aside, the time came for me to meet the mystery man. If my *coiffure* and bulky shoulder immobilizer didn't scare him away, I was confident that I could present my evidence in a convincing fashion.

The 10-minute ride from my home to the local Panera restaurant seemed to take hours. Impending doom has a way of making time slow down. Just as an accident victim senses the immediate crash and all the gory details in high-definition slow motion, I felt that my six-mile journey to a lunch appointment would change my life forever. Holding my phone in my left hand, I kept fidgeting with the keypad as my husband drove under the speed limit to our destination.

"What are you doing?" he asked.

"I'm trying to figure out a series of numbers that I can discreetly text you with only my left hand, in case things don't go well—an SOS text. I need a plan in case they shove me in the trunk. When you drop me off, don't go back home; stay close in case I need to be rescued. Drive over to the next parking lot and just hang out. If something happens, I'll send the SOS code. It's 1-7-7-7."

My husband didn't bat an eye or turn his head toward me. After about a minute of silence, during which I assumed he was thinking about fishing or something equally earth-shattering, he finally said, "I think you're blowing this out of proportion."

"You won't say that when I don't come home tonight. Do you remember the code?"

"Yes, it's 9-8-7-6." Before I could grab the door handle with my left hand to open the car door and fling myself onto the pavement, he said, "Yes, I remember. It's 1-7-7-7."

Looking calm and walking confidently with a cell phone tucked into the sleeve of my shoulder immobilizer while carrying a plain manila envelope with enough evidence to disrupt a corporation was no easy feat, but I managed to pull it off. I immediately spotted the mysterious lawyer—straight out of *L.A. Law*, sitting alone at a table in a dark blue suit and tie.

There was no attempted kidnapping, no bodies stuffed in a trunk, and no murder. The lawyer seemed genuine and sincerely impressed with the documentation as well as my presentation of the facts. The next step would be a second meeting with yet another lawyer and the necessary and unpleasant task of contract signing. I didn't have to use the SOS code, and I breathed a sigh of relief. But I had no way of knowing that serious threats to my personal safety would materialize with time and haunt me for years to come.

Truth Beside Me

DO NOT ENTER.
A warning? A threat?
I feel compelled to enter.
Truth, beside me, silent.

A rule follower,
Not a rule breaker.
But I cannot look away.
Truth, beside me, said nothing.

DO NOT OPEN.
Fear, hesitation, and doubt
Fill my head.
Truth, beside me, said go in.

I know no one
Who has crossed this threshold.
I am alone.
Walk away or walk through?

My life will change forever.
Truth extends her hand.
I walk through,
Truth beside me.

(July 2014, before meeting with the lawyer for the first time)

CHAPTER 2

Misneach

"Without belittling the courage with which men have died,
we should not forget those acts of courage with which men ...
have lived. The courage of life is often a less dramatic
spectacle than the courage of a final moment, but it is no less
a magnificent mixture of triumph and tragedy."
—John Fitzgerald Kennedy (1917–1963)

Perhaps it's in my genes. According to my genetic profile, I am 67% Scots-Irish. I am intrigued with the Celtic heritage and language. The lush green landscapes and craggy wild shores of the Irish coastline have beckoned me for many years. My father's Scottish ancestors immigrated to the eastern North Carolina coast from Ayrshire, the home of Scotland's national poet, Robert Burns. As a Burns myself, my penchant for storytelling may have originated in that land of rugged highlands, historic castles, and stunning landscapes. My red hair, freckled skin, and light-colored eyes connect me to the culture. My independent spirit, self-reliance, and resilience tie me emotionally to my ancestors. My inner *Braveheart* is most decidedly a Scots-Irish quality wrapped in an Irish Gaelic word, *misneach*, meaning courage, bravery, fortitude, and a quiet sense of strength.

The theme of courage has woven through my life with weighty expectations. I admire those who take chances, do heroic things, and overcome the odds. My father was an Air Force veteran, my brother an Army veteran, and my father-in-law a Navy veteran. My father and father-in-law were not ones to openly discuss their experiences until their later years. What they endured defending our country, our lives, our families, and our freedoms, including my freedom to tell my story, was the worst of war and the worst of humanity, and yet they managed to maintain positive attitudes and create fulfilling lives: that is true courage and remarkable resilience. That is *misneach*.

Following my graduation from the University of Virginia, I stood on the steps of the Navy recruiting office in Charlottesville, Virginia, and wondered if I was brave enough to enlist in the armed forces. I was not. I never walked through that door. Fear of the unknown made me turn around. At about that same time, the National Security Agency recruited me as a linguist because I had strong foreign language skills, but once again, I was not brave enough to follow that path. The disappointment in myself for not stepping into either one of those adventurous roles settled deeply into my psyche. I vowed that if I were ever again presented with the opportunity to be courageous, I would take it and not let fear of the unknown control me.

I worked briefly in the world of scientific research and publication at the Medical College of Virginia. The rigors of neuroanatomy experiments and academic publication suited my desire for meaningful, challenging work, but the paycheck for such lofty ideals barely kept me alive. Without a car, my commute to downtown work depended on the public transit service or my bicycle. Riding my 10-speed Schwinn to work through city traffic was neither adventurous nor safe. I often didn't have the toll money to cross the inaptly named Nickel Bridge, so I would pedal faster as I approached the toll booth. Thankfully, no one ever complained about my freeloading.

Determined to make a better life for myself, I decided a higher-paying profession would put me on the right path. A friend suggested pharmaceutical sales would suit my scientific brain and generate a much better paycheck. So, I threw myself into finding the perfect pharmaceutical job even though I had zero knowledge or connections. Not knowing where to begin, I looked for help from the university librarian, who pointed me to the Thomas Register of American Manufacturers: massive volumes of U.S. manufacturers with information on CEOs, products, and services. I spent hours taking notes on companies whose names sounded familiar: Glaxo, Merck, Roche, and Johnson & Johnson. Then I wrote directly to the CEO of each company requesting an interview.

Misneach!

As expected, almost no one answered, and a few redirected me to someone else who also didn't answer. More than a little discouraged, I thought I'd never escape what I now considered drudgery in the laboratory. But after several months, I received a letter from Hoffmann-LaRoche inviting me to an interview with a local sales manager. Elated, I knew that this was my one opportunity to positively change my life. I prepared for weeks—a professional-looking suit, nicer shoes than I was accustomed to, and a not-too-feminine bag for carrying two copies of my freshly typed résumé. The only potential pitfall was my hunk-of-junk rebuilt Honda that was affordable but unreliable and prone to overheating.

Interview day unfolded worse than I could have imagined. With the Honda sputtering all the way to the interview, I was distracted and missed the exit to a local Hyatt hotel lobby where the interview was scheduled. "No problem," I told myself, because a big perk of pharmaceutical sales jobs was a car, and that was something I desperately needed. In fact, if the interviewer had offered me a car and no paycheck, I would probably have accepted. I had more than enough time to make a U-turn at the next light and drive the one and a half miles to the hotel. Then, as if God himself were testing me, the car engine started to smoke and died—a complete and absolute death.

Feeling close to hopeless, I hopped out of the expired car and walked the one and a half miles in the biting February wind to make it to the interview on time. I looked Mr. Williams in the eye, shook his hand, gave him the unwrinkled copy of my résumé, and excused myself to call a tow truck. Despite the disastrous start to the day, I got the job and worked for Hoffmann-LaRoche for 17 years. Many years later, Mr. Williams confided that my dogged determination to make it to our first interview convinced him that I could handle anything.

Misneach!

Over the next several decades, I acquired a husband, three stepchildren, two children, six dogs, and a successful 33-year sales career in the pharmaceutical industry. I was busy creating a life and raising a family.

The corporate pharmaceutical world was changing rapidly during that time. The companies were expanding exponentially and buying out the smaller ones. Competition became cutthroat, and layoffs were routine, especially after 2000. It was during this time that the pressure-cooker world of sales exploded. Rumors swirled weekly in companies large and small about buyouts and downsizing. Questionable sales tactics emerged and then took hold of the industry like a rapidly growing, incurable cancer. Everyone in the industry knew it and felt it. Almost every single person remained silently complicit about the unethical, yet wholly accepted, strategies of paying off doctors to prescribe products; providing lavish vacations for "high prescribers" and their spouses; and offering exorbitant speakers' fees to entice the highest potential prescribers to convince others to do the same. It was one gigantic Ponzi scheme with the potential for all the players to benefit financially—unless, of course, you had any sense of morals or honesty.

Everyone knew the rules of the game. Sales goals skyrocketed annually, and so did the pressure on sales representatives to smash those goals quarter after quarter, year after year. The constant chatter of layoffs droned on like a low hum in the background. Those who didn't want to play the game were predictably and swiftly given the boot. Monetary goals were established using questionable metrics and complicated calculations that even the managers couldn't fully explain to their teams. Those who exceeded goals were handsomely rewarded with money, trips, and promotions. To reach their goals, nothing was considered off-limits, unethical, or illegal.

At the predictably ostentatious annual national sales meeting, representatives would dutifully nod while administrative staff in the compliance department warned us of the dire consequences of off-label marketing: $250,000 in fines per occurrence, jail time, and FDA representatives lurking in doctors' offices waiting to overhear representatives sharing incorrect information. Those warnings would quickly fade away during the next session, which would glamorize and reward those within the corporation who had, in effect, ignored all the compliance rules and smashed all of their goals—it was a reason to celebrate. The dichotomy was breathtaking, and not in a good way.

At the age of 50, following another corporate layoff, I was hired as an experienced representative for a new company specializing in pain management. I felt very fortunate and grateful to have been offered the position at my age. The pharmaceutical world is full of the young and beautiful. I didn't fit that profile, but I had what they needed: I knew the job, the territory, and the customers. My date of hire was August 10, 2011. Unbeknownst to me at the time, this was the beginning of my decade-plus battle.

Perfect

Now that you are ours
You must speak with these words
These perfect words
And only these words.

And when you speak
In perfect sentences
You must use perfect transitions
Because the words must flow.

You must practice again, AGAIN!
Until these perfect words,
Sentences, transitions, and phrases
Roll off your now forked tongue.

If you do not conform
To the perfect way,
We will cheerfully ruin you
Because, remember, you are ours.

We will demean, humiliate, isolate,
Ridicule and gaslight until you break.
Only the perfect will survive
In our world of perfect lies.

(February 2012, one and a half years into Depomed
employment)

CHAPTER 3

Déjà Vu

"Time is a figure eight,
at its center the city of Déjà Vu."
—Robert Breault

I sat in the Philadelphia airport hotel lobby eyeing my competition: a virtual city of smartly dressed young professionals, all vying for coveted sales positions in the startup pharmaceutical company Depomed. Startup companies with new and exciting products always attract the most well-groomed and confident applicant pool. The pressure-cooker atmosphere added to my already bubbling age insecurity. I would turn 50 in less than two weeks. I recall thinking how young and beautiful they looked, and that made me sweat.

However, I had a plan.

It was late morning before I was called for my interview in a nondescript hotel meeting room with a large, friendly man named Dudley. *This is a positive sign,* I thought to myself; he had the same name as the friendly guardian angel from the classic film *The Bishop's Wife*. So, I said a little prayer that my guardian angel would be watching over me, too. The usual line of questioning began—experience, results, etc.—questions I expected and had been answering for so many years. And then came the one that would make or break me. But I was prepared for it.

"So, what makes you qualified for this job over everyone else who is here today?" Dudley asked.

I don't know how to play the actual board game of chess, but I like to imagine myself as a finalist in the *life* game of chess. I'd planned this several moves in advance. Without missing a beat, I reached into my bag, pulled out a stack of well-worn business cards, and slid them across the table. I gave Dudley a minute to digest the significance of my handwritten notes scrawled all over the cards: best hours to contact, names of key office staff, lunch preferences. He seemed a little slow on the uptake. "The names on those cards," I told him, "are probable targets for the new product the company will be launching in October."

His eyes lit up.

Checkmate!

My previous experience as a pharmaceutical representative was clearly a factor in Depomed's interest in me. Several years before, I'd been hired by Endo, a company specializing in the pain drugs Lidoderm and Opana ER, an extended-release oxymorphone. Not long into the launch of Opana ER, there was talk of marketing it as an abuse deterrent, making it the safest opioid on the market. If that information had been true, it would have been a breakthrough in the pain management market. But there was no scientific evidence to support that claim. I had refused to discuss the anti-abuse potential in my sales calls, and management did not like my stance. Some months later, during my mid-year review, the manager looked me in the eyes and flatly said, "You know that no one likes you."

That curveball out of left field stung. I had no response. I just stared at him while trying to process what I had just heard. Corporate gaslighting at Endo had officially begun, and I knew my days there were numbered.

To add insult to injury, one of my teammates' over-the-top aggressive marketing tactics with Lidoderm generated daily customer complaints. I was constantly putting out fires wherever he had been. Humiliated and demoralized, I spent the greater part of every day apologizing for his behavior. Because I'm a strong advocate for the Golden Rule, I believed everyone deserved to be treated with respect, not just those who could write prescriptions. I brought my concerns to management and later to human resources. Unfortunately, the tables turned on me, and I was the one they chose to investigate. In hindsight, I should have been more savvy about the connection between my co-worker and the manager. They were behaviorally identical: manipulative and deceitful, embodying the phrase "the end justifies the means," and to hell with whatever truth or person blocked their path.

As with most situations that are uncomfortable, I learned an enormously valuable lesson. Confiding in HR was a poor move on my part, and I would not make the same mistake again. What I didn't know at the time was that human resources has the dubious reputation of earmarking employees who speak up as potential trouble for the company, and in some cases, the label is extrapolated to mean potential whistleblower. Moral of the story: HR protects the company, not the employee.

As a side note, in 2014, Endo was fined $192.7 million by the Department of Justice for off-label marketing of Lidoderm. The fallout continued in 2024 when Endo was fined $1.5 *billion* for deceptively marketing Opana ER and their role in the opioid crisis. This was the second-largest set of criminal financial penalties ever levied against a pharmaceutical company. My intuition had never been wrong, and this confirmed my suspicions.

After receiving the heave-ho at Endo, I was glad to be free of that cesspool of liars and miscreants. Sweet revenge came in the form of a fabulous job offer from Adolor as a senior hospital account executive, a valuable promotion in the pharmaceutical industry hierarchy. The hospital environment is a political hotbed, but if you can survive there, you can survive just about anywhere in the pharma world. Hospital representatives who do well in the job are always prime picking for other companies. Nationally ranked number two in the company, I was proud of my accomplishments, but tensions flared once again. I was constantly at odds with Glaxo reps with whom Adolor co-marketed Entereg, an abdominal surgical pain product. Their unscrupulous sales tactics and nasty attitude toward me when I refused to join them left me once again questioning my reason for staying in pharma sales.

My increasing disillusion and dissatisfaction with the industry continued to climb. But I set my gut instincts aside (bad idea!) and remained in the pharmaceutical industry because I had a track record of success and, quite honestly, didn't know what else I could do with my life. I noticed a pattern was beginning to emerge: was I the problem, or were the pharma companies morphing into the greedy, unethical giants that the majority of healthcare providers already assumed them to be?

As I sat thinking about this in that dreary Philadelphia airport hotel lobby, waiting for the second round of interviews, I strategically placed myself in a large comfy armchair where I had a good view of my competition. While I pretended to read *The Wall Street Journal*, I tried to discern who my competition was for the position I was interviewing for. It didn't take long to narrow it down to a handsome young man in his early 30s with a confident air about him—bad news for me. He 100% looked and acted the part of Mr. GQ Pharma Representative. Before I could drown myself too deeply in my own pity party, I was called for the second interview with Paul, a polite, elderly gentleman whose title was Mid-Atlantic Regional Sales Director.

Getting right to the point, Paul asked, "So I hear you know Dr. Hancock. How well do you know him?"

I quickly figured out that he'd got this information from guardian angel Dudley and the stack of business cards I'd presented in the first interview.

"Yes, I worked with him while I was at Endo. He was a high-writing prescriber."

I was curious. Why was this second interview revolving entirely around Dr. Hancock? But then I made the connection: Dr. Hancock had already been identified by Depomed as a target (a potential high prescriber) for their new gabapentin product, Gralise. My instincts were 100% on point.

Paul offered me the job, and as he gripped my hand tightly, he said, "You know, Hancock can put you on the map." I smiled and thanked him for the opportunity, but a vague dark feeling settled over me. As I was leaving, Paul congratulated me once again and winked as he said, "Faith, family, and then work. That's what it's all about."

I remember thinking how unusual it was that someone in the pharma industry would utter those words, introducing faith into the conversation. As I left for the airport to fly back home, I replayed Paul's parting comments in my mind.

"Maybe this company will be different after all," I told my husband when I called him with the good news of my job offer, and the optimistic thought that Depomed could turn out to be an ethical pharmaceutical company. That was August 10, 2011.

Within 2.5 weeks, on August 29, 2011, I received a phone call from Paul. Although brief, I knew I had misjudged the ethics of Depomed.

When I picked up the phone, Hurricane Irene was howling outside my home office windows. A large and destructive tropical cyclone, her fury coincided with mine as I listened to Paul asking me to do a favor for him. Although I was hired on August 10, I didn't officially begin until September. With the trees violently bending in the heavy rain and wind, I tried to calm both the dreaded voice in my head and my frightened Great Dane, who was watching the storm with me from my office on the third floor.

Despite his half-hearted attempt at small talk and thinly veiled excuse of checking on me during the storm, I suspected this call was about something else entirely, and my suspicion was correct. Paul asked me to invite Dr. Hancock and his wife to the upcoming Gralise launch meeting in San Diego in October. Not wanting to immediately be labeled as an employee who "doesn't play well with others in the sandbox," I reluctantly agreed. The worst part was not that he requested my effort before I was officially on board, but that his request was illegal! By 2011, it was well understood that inviting spouses on trips could create a financial relationship prohibited under multiple federal laws, like the Anti-Kickback Statute, which prohibits offering remuneration to influence referrals.

Decades of lavish pharmaceutical inducements had garnered so much deserved negative press that by late 2008, Pharmaceutical Research and Manufacturers of America (PhRMA) voluntarily revised its code of conduct, banning reminder items and other gifts to physicians. Pens, notepads, and other swag with company logos were discontinued due to the possibility of subliminally influencing doctors' prescribing habits. Not fully convinced that pharmaceutical companies could reliably police themselves, the Sunshine Act of 2010 was codified as part of the Affordable Care Act. Using the metaphor of sunshine as the best disinfectant against corruption, the name reflects the belief that public scrutiny, like the light of the sun, can prevent "ineptitude, negligence, and corruption" by making actions visible to the public.

Manufacturers and group purchasing organizations (GPOs) were required to report payments greater than $10 made to physicians for consulting, speaking engagements, research, and royalties to the Centers for Medicare & Medicaid Services (CMS). This information was then made available to the public to increase transparency and uncover potential conflicts of interest.

By September 2011, when Paul directed me to invite Dr. Hancock and his wife to San Diego for "a nice getaway," as he phrased it, there were no fewer than 10 published acts, guidelines, compliance manuals, and codes on interactions and ethics concerning pharmaceutical companies, clearly defined for the industry. That one single call violated every one of them. I would be directed by both my immediate managers and the Mid-Atlantic Regional Sales Director to make this same offer to Dr. Hancock on at least a half dozen occasions over the next two years.

FIRE

They will burn you
It won't be quick
Or a blaze of glory
A slow, torturous burn.

You will know it.
At first, you will be strong.
Adrenaline masks the pain.
Then you will feel it.

Inch by inch,
Organ by organ,
You will be consumed.
Now it hurts

Almost nothing is left,
Except the truth.
It will extinguish the flame
Eventually.

(April 13, 2013, Depomed retaliation has begun)

CHAPTER 4

Orphans and Cannibals

"A lie which is half a truth is ever the blackest of lies." —**Alfred, Lord Tennyson**

Before I dive headfirst into the subsequent tumultuous two years, I need to lay a bit of groundwork. This is the backstory.

In 2011, the FDA approved Depomed's Gralise (gabapentin tablets) for the once-daily treatment of post-herpetic neuralgia (PHN). PHN is the chronic, lingering neuropathic pain following herpes zoster, commonly known as shingles. The comprehensive research, development, and approval process to bring a new drug to the U.S. market can take an astonishing 12 to 15 years. But the timeline for Depomed was significantly shorter due to multiple factors. Gabapentin, the active ingredient in Gralise, had already been in clinical trials for various uses since the 1980s. The immediate-release form of gabapentin (Neurontin) was first approved in the U.S. for epilepsy in 1993, and later for

PHN in May 2002. In November 2008, Depomed entered a license agreement with Solvay Pharmaceuticals for the extended-release formulation of gabapentin.

Depomed relied on the previous research and track record of generic gabapentin, thus reducing the expense and time normally required to bring a new drug to market. And then came the final golden egg, which additionally sped up the approval timeline: the FDA designated Gralise as an orphan drug for the management of PHN in November 2010.

An orphan drug is a medication developed to treat a rare disease or condition, often because traditional market incentives are insufficient. Gralise obtained full approval on January 28, 2011, a mere three years after obtaining the drug from Solvay.

Orphan drug designation comes with a goldmine of benefits for companies whose products meet the definition of a rare disease, namely, prevalence in fewer than 200,000 individuals in the United States. Once that hurdle is cleared, financial and regulatory benefits follow, including seven years of market exclusivity in the U.S., tax credits for qualified clinical trials, and waivers for user fees. It also provides regulatory support, such as scientific advice from the FDA, which can help lower development costs and increase the funding potential.

The orphan drug status of Gralise was contested for years by the FDA, the same organization that granted the initial golden egg in the first place. The controversy centered around the clinical superiority of Gralise to gabapentin. Depomed initially obtained orphan drug designation for Gralise by arguing it was for a rare disease, PHN, and had a lower incidence of side effects than immediate-release versions of the same active ingredient, gabapentin. However, the FDA later contested granting Gralise orphan drug exclusivity after its approval, arguing that because the active ingredient, gabapentin, was the same as Neurontin (also approved for PHN) and not proven to be clinically superior, it was not entitled to the seven-year marketing exclusivity. Depomed sued the FDA, and in 2014, a federal district court ordered the FDA to grant the exclusivity, stating the Orphan Drug Act required it for any drug with a prior orphan designation and marketing approval. Despite losing the Gralise case, the FDA issued a policy clarification stating the court's ruling was specific to Gralise, and the agency would continue to apply its interpretation that a drug must show clinical superiority to receive exclusivity if it is the same drug as a previously approved one.

While the clinical superiority of Gralise took center stage legally, that battle was quiet and hushed. But excitement grew with the marketing arm of Depomed as they hired 164 field sales representatives dedicated to promoting its flagship product, Gralise. Newly hired representatives, including me, prepared for the upcoming launch meeting through online modules about disease state, drug pharmacodynamics, marketing, and lists of primary care physicians who would become our first customers. During this intensive training, we were often reminded about the one million shingles patients that would soon benefit from Gralise. But there was a potential problem in this message: the drug we were about to launch was not for shingles; it had been approved for one indication only: post-herpetic neuralgia.

Post-herpetic neuralgia is generally thought to afflict 10–15% of shingles patients. That equates to approximately 100,000–150,000 cases total per year, right in line with the orphan drug guidelines. Another significant but rarely mentioned detail during our training was the fact that in 2006, five years prior to the launch of Gralise, the first shingles vaccine, Zostavax, was introduced. With proven efficacy at reducing shingles and post-herpetic neuralgia, the incidence of both was in steep decline. In studying the details of the product and disease state, I was already connecting the puzzle pieces. Depomed planned to enter a declining disease market, one with less than 200,000 patients per year, where a generic and effective drug therapy already existed. This made no sense.

But the clues to this riddle were hiding in plain sight. During this same time frame, the sales of generic gabapentin had been rising exponentially. Gabapentin was introduced into the market in the 1990s for seizures and PHN, but physicians quickly adopted it for a broad range of off-label uses: diabetic neuropathy, fibromyalgia, anxiety disorders, insomnia, chronic pain, and hot flashes, to name a few.

Off-label drug use refers to the practice of prescribing a drug for a different purpose than the FDA approval. Physicians commonly prescribe drugs outside of approved indications, and the FDA's longstanding position is that physicians can legally prescribe drugs off-label based on their clinical judgment. On the other hand, manufacturers cannot market or promote these uses. It is illegal under the Federal Food, Drug, and Cosmetic Act (FD&C Act) for pharmaceutical companies and their representatives to proactively promote drugs for off-label uses not approved by the FDA. This practice is considered misbranding, and the FDA can take regulatory and enforcement action, often resulting in significant fines and legal settlements.

This is Pharma 101. Every single pharmaceutical company and representative is fully aware of the illegality of off-label promotion, but it is despicably routine and casts a long shadow across the integrity of the industry as a whole. One of the pharmaceutical industry's most protected secrets, off-label promotion is underhandedly incorporated into the fabric of pharma companies, specifically factored into ever-increasing sales goals. Silence about the secret is rewarded. Achievers or offenders, depending on one's perspective, are handsomely rewarded with bigger paychecks, bonuses, and lavish trips.

If a representative wants to consistently rise to the top of the leader board, an element of off-label promotion is most likely taking place. Company leadership is the guilty guiding hand behind this scenario, considering any resulting fines as the cost of doing business. For confirmation of this playbook, look no further than pharmaceutical giants like Pfizer, Johnson & Johnson, and GlaxoSmithKline that have faced multiple fines for repeated off-label promotion.

So what was the Depomed-Gralise connection to the playbook? The future of the product and the company was dependent on a half-truth: Gralise could replace gabapentin for whatever a doctor wanted to prescribe it for.

An expensive branded product was about to be launched in an orphan drug market where the incidence of disease was declining, but the generic drug market was rising. Depomed's goal was obvious: get the drug approved quickly; protect and extend the patent exclusivity through orphan drug status; and quietly expand off-label sales to cannibalize the generic gabapentin market. Deceptively genius!

One detail, though, would prove to be more than a minor inconvenience. The final package insert approved by the FDA specifically stated that "Gralise is not interchangeable with other gabapentin products because of differing pharmacokinetic profiles that affect the frequency of administration."

The FDA had effectively legally squashed any cannibalization of the generic market with one sentence. This would prove to be Depomed's Achilles heel and the basis of future litigation.

Corporate Graffiti

Plans, presentations, projections
Overflowing with lies.
You created the graffiti
And expected me to cheerfully spread it,
Like manure in the field.

I will not be happily complicit;
I will not be silently complicit;
I will NOT be indifferent.

But I WILL silently conserve it.
Charts, conversations, contests, and communications
Preserved, locked away, copied,
Duplicated and password protected.

Now the confidentials
Displayed for the world to witness
Your greed, your threats, your corruption
Your clandestine graffiti
Has now become
Evidence.

(November 30, 2014, one month after the first federal *qui tam*
False Claims Act lawsuit was filed)

CHAPTER 5

Dirty Money

*"One of the truest tests of integrity is
its blunt refusal to be compromised."*
—Chinua Achebe

It was a beautiful Southern California day in early October 2011. The weather was cool with early morning clouds giving way to partly sunny skies, and the mood was electric. After weeks of home study, the Gralise launch meeting in San Diego had finally arrived. I had attended many launch meetings in my pharmaceutical career, and this one followed the same itinerary: over-the-top productions designed to be motivational and energizing, and events that prompted the new sales force to get out there and sell a drug, which would lead to higher profits. Each day was rigidly scheduled with meetings and breakout sessions from morning through evening. Following the requisite 7 a.m. breakfast, meetings kicked off promptly, with loud music, blaring lights, and high-profile company directors babbling motivational clichés at their audience. While some representatives thrived in this atmosphere, I wasn't one of them. In fact, I dreaded launch meetings, primarily because they showcased the superficiality of the industry: glitz, glamour, and dirty money were layered on thick, while concern for the patient was relegated to a much lower level of importance.

In this fishbowl of nerves and anticipation, most of the new hires wanted to impress management with their good looks and sales skills. The scene reminded me of a feeding frenzy of sharks when chum is thrown into the water. As the sales director climbed onto the stage for the inaugural session, his "chum" was a challenge to the eager sharks in front of him.

"Who's going to sell 100 prescriptions of Gralise in week one? Stand up!"

Representatives cheered wildly and clapped like trained seals. Some stood up. I remained seated, feeling an ache in the pit of my stomach.

"Keep standing," he continued. "Who is going to sell 90 prescriptions in week one? Stand up!"

He continued: "Who's going to sell 80 prescriptions—70—60—50—until the few people who were still sitting, me included, finally relented and stood up at the 40 prescription mark. As I rose slowly to my feet, the colleague next to me did the same, and we shot each other a knowing look. Gralise was an orphan drug with a niche indication. If anyone achieved five prescriptions a week, it would be a miracle.

In that first hour of the first day, the charade that had just played out answered the question I had spent weeks mulling over in my mind: was the company going to promote this product ethically within the guidelines of the package insert, or unethically, outside of the package insert? The resounding response of "unethical promotion" throbbed in my head like a migraine.

Unrealistically high sales expectations were the order of the day once we returned home to our appointed territories. At first, the managerial messages sounded somewhat motivational, then became desperate, and later threatening. By mid-December 2011, barely two months after the launch meeting, Depomed management was clearly disappointed in the lack of sales. Accusations, finger-pointing, and rumors of layoffs began to swirl just as the unfestive Christmas holiday was beginning. While this was not a new phenomenon in the pharmaceutical world when sales waned, I had never seen it materialize so quickly. As early as January 2012, representatives were fired due to anemic sales. Colleagues turned on each other to defend their sales in relation to those of others within the same division.

To quell the rebellion, or perhaps hasten the end, Depomed management abandoned its previous sales target list and established sales goals. Primary care physicians, who treat the bulk of patients with shingles, were not writing the volume of prescriptions that Depomed anticipated. To overcome this obstacle, each representative was assigned a new list of physicians, known as targets, heavily weighted with those involved in pain management. These new targets, Depomed reasoned, wrote large quantities of gabapentin prescriptions, and so they would be easy money for the company. All representatives were now directed to move their messaging away from the indication of post-herpetic neuralgia and concentrate their calls on the switch from generic gabapentin to the more convenient once-daily Gralise. To add weight and motivation to this new campaign, each representative was assigned sales goals, and their compensation was dependent on reaching them.

The new business plan made sense monetarily, but legally and ethically, it was a minefield. If you recall, the Gralise package insert specifically stated that generic gabapentin and Gralise were not interchangeable due to differing pharmacokinetic profiles. Directing representatives to fall in line with the new business plan was basically directing us to break the law. To jump-start the new plan, Depomed created monetary incentives for representatives for increasing the volume of prescriptions—higher-strength prescriptions and higher refill rates—and generating new physician customers. Each parameter would generate a higher bonus payout and more positive recognition for representatives. Fun contest names like March Madness, complete with tournament-style elimination brackets, were meant to increase the competitive feeling among the sales force. In reality, there was nothing fun or lighthearted about it. In my opinion, Depomed was breaking the law, pure and simple, and expected representatives to fall in line. Almost everyone did, with one notable exception: me.

Selling pain management drugs carries a higher responsibility than selling other drugs because of the risk of abuse and diversion. Gabapentin is not an opioid, and for that reason, many physicians relied on its pain relief profile rather than prescribing opioids. They felt it was safe, offered a low risk profile, and as one physician told me, "No one's going to 'off' themselves with it." But that's not the entire story on gabapentin. In many states, it is considered a "drug of concern." When used with other central nervous system depressants such as opioids, there is a risk for respiratory depression, potentially resulting in death. The percentage of deaths where gabapentin is detected that were opioid-involved remains consistently high, ranging from 85–90%. Gabapentin in all forms remains overprescribed in large part due to pharmaceutical companies, like Depomed, incentivizing representatives to sell larger quantities in higher-dosage strengths and with multiple refills. It is not a harmless drug, and the large quantities that remain unused in medicine cabinets across the country are ripe for diversion and abuse.

This was never a point of discussion with Gralise. Depomed concentrated solely on churning out prescriptions and raking in profits. The few times that I mentioned side effects, managers came down hard on me, questioning why I would even bring it up. I would half-sarcastically refer them to Gralise's package insert.

Field rides are a common practice in the pharmaceutical industry. Managers spend a day or two in the field with representatives to be sure that all protocols are correctly followed and that product information conveyed to the physician is accurate and compliant. During a field ride with my manager, Dudley, I questioned him on the calculation of sales goals.

"How were the sales goals calculated? They look high considering the incidence of shingles and PHN is so small. Every physician has told me that they rarely treat PHN, and the most that they see is one or two cases per year.”

Dudley fumbled for a minute or two and finally settled on the usual dodgeball answer, “If that’s what the home office says, then that’s what it is.”

“Lemming,” I thought to myself. But I wanted a real answer, so I rephrased my question. “It looks to me like generic gabapentin is incorporated into the sales goals.”

“It probably is,” Dudley responded quickly.

Just as quickly, I interjected that this was not a valid calculation because generic gabapentin is used for so many off-label indications. “If you are expecting me to sell Gralise for off-label indications, that is not right, and I won’t do it. I’ll stick to the package insert.”

When the day with Dudley had concluded, I took copious notes on that conversation, realizing it was the first solid admission of Depomed’s fraudulent marketing scheme. That scenario would play out time and time again—questions, admissions, and note-taking. These handwritten contemporaneous notes would later be entered into evidence in the first whistleblower complaint filed against Depomed and investigated by the Department of Justice.

My personal reconnaissance mission had officially begun. Handwritten notes on scraps of paper, and emails and marketing plans discussing generic gabapentin filled a miscellaneous folder labeled “Miscellaneous,” a purposefully bland name for the mounting evidence I was accumulating. Sales projections and goals, sales scenarios, and investor presentations touting the success of Depomed cannibalizing the generic market rounded out my evidence file. I had incriminating and irrefutable data.

I sensed I was being labeled as a troublemaker, which, though not unexpected, felt very uncomfortable. I was being noticed by Depomed managers. In March 2012, the Mid-Atlantic Regional Sales Manager (Paul) scheduled a field ride with me. It was like being called into the principal's office, and I knew that it was not going to go well. I steeled myself to accept that I would likely be fired that day, but I knew that whatever happened, I would not compromise my integrity or my stance on unscrupulous marketing. If I were pushed to do so, I knew I would resign immediately. I thought about how my life would change and how I would support my family with no income. The end of my professional career was at hand. I picked Paul up from the hotel at 6:30 a.m. The pleasantries lasted less than a minute.

Taking charge of my fate, I confidently told Paul, "I'm assuming you're here to fire me today. Why don't you just do it now and save us both the time and the pretense?" I felt like I was asking the executioner to carry out his duty.

"I'm not here to fire you. Let's get on with our day," he remarked, grinning smugly.

His response seemed vague, insincere, and came too quickly, almost as if he had anticipated I would call for my own demise, or as if he would relish watching me self-destruct. Mercifully, the day concluded with no dramatic ending, but I couldn't ignore the tugging of an ocean riptide waiting to suck me under.

The pressure to meet ever-increasing sales goals continued to ratchet up. Off-label promotion was not specifically discussed but was openly incorporated into sales goals. Depomed was unapologetically laser-focused on the highest gabapentin writers. Any discussion of PHN was in the rearview mirror. This glaring omission was occasionally rationalized with the comment, "If you have ever mentioned PHN in a previous sales call, it is not necessary to bring it up again." How convenient that the talking point didn't apply to the mention of replacing generic gabapentin with Gralise. No physician specialty was off limits—anyone and everyone who wrote gabapentin prescriptions was a potential customer.

In my entire pharmaceutical career, I had never been a part of such unscrupulous marketing. Case in point: Orthopedic physicians prescribe a high volume of gabapentin but do not treat PHN patients *per se*. During a field ride with my manager, I drove past a high-rise office complex with a large business marquee visible from the interstate: "Orthopaedic and Spine Specialists." Dudley rubbed his hands together and licked his lips as if he were about to devour a ribeye steak.

"Why are you driving past that office?" he asked me, still rubbing his palms together.

"Because they don't treat patients with PHN," I answered flatly.

"Are they on your target list?"

I took a deep breath, hoping it would help calm my rattled nerves, as I already knew the direction of this conversation. "Yes, they are, but they shouldn't be because they don't treat PHN. I won't talk off-label."

The same tired response from Dudley: "If the home office has assigned those doctors to you, then you have to go in there."

The topic and the circular conversation reared their boorish heads time after time. The tension in the car was palpable. Once he left for the day, I made notes, adding them to my growing Miscellaneous file.

By October 2012, insurance companies and the federal government took notice of the growing expenditure on Gralise and put their collective foot down. Most companies would now only green-light it for the approved indication, PHN, but that could have been a death knell for Gralise. However, there was a loophole. If a patient could not tolerate generic gabapentin, or if other therapies had been unsuccessful, Gralise would be approved, and insurance companies would once again pay. This is called "step-editing," and it is standard practice with insurance companies and high-priced therapies.

It was not unexpected news, but the new, tighter approval regulations were announced while we attended a national meeting, and Depomed's response was sheer panic. The noose was tightening around the company's neck. While they had made substantial inroads with all physician specialties through off-label marketing, this would surely throw a wrench in their future sales data. It was time once again for a new corporate marketing plan.

But meanwhile, in an odd turn of events, sales in my territory increased rather than decreased. The uptick in my territory's sales could be traced to one pain management physician affiliated with a pain clinic in Washington, D.C. Coincidentally, he and his colleagues had been on the Gralise research team prior to its launch in 2011. Physicians involved in pre-launch drug research very often become the most prolific prescribers of the new product and quite often become paid speakers on behalf of the company. This particular physician had already devised a workaround to skirt the insurance companies' upcoming squeeze on reimbursement and was successfully getting reimbursement for all types of indications. Depomed wanted to know how and why this was working so that they could relay the details to physicians all over the country.

Depomed management was furious with me because I didn't know, or want to know, the scheme the physician was using, and they were also fuming because Dr. Hancock, my original contact when I was hired, would not get on board the Gralise train. As a result, Depomed was weighing its options on how much longer it would tolerate my insolence, or integrity, depending on one's perspective.

As the end of the year approached, layoffs and territory realignments once again became the stuff of spicy rumors. Dudley had assured me several times that my territory would not be realigned and that I was safe from reorganization. On January 1, 2013, I was transferred to a new division, with a headquarters city three hours from my home and a manager from hell (MFH). The deceit and manipulation intensified as I realized there was a concerted campaign to oust me, and it started from the top. My days at Depomed were numbered.

Pharmaceutical companies typically convene a sales meeting in January to bring everyone together, slap each other on the back, and hold an awards dinner to recognize top sales performers from the previous year. It's a time for team building and setting direction for the upcoming year. Depomed's January 2013 meeting was a bright red warning signal.

Having worked in team structures for decades, I'd noticed an interesting but constant phenomenon emerging: one person within the group has access to higher-ups as well as the latest gossip. Dan was that person in my group, so at break time we'd convene around the coffee table and swap stories. Word of my relocation had spread like wildfire, and he was the first to broach the still-sore topic with me.

"I heard your territory was realigned," Dan began. "Sorry to hear that. We're going to miss you."

Feeling utterly dejected, all I could muster was, "Thanks. I'll miss you guys, too."

He continued, "Dudley told me they did it to teach you a lesson. To warn you to keep your mouth shut."

Those words felt like a bullet piercing my body. They confirmed the deliberate and planned corporate attack against me. "They" included the Mid-Atlantic Regional Sales Director, who had spent a field day with me in March 2012. His intention was now crystal clear: he planned to coordinate and witness my self-destruction.

The highlight and conclusion of the day was an hours-long awards dinner. My former teammates sat huddled together at their dinner table, congratulating their manager, Dudley, who received an award. His success was due entirely to the sales performance of two of his team members, and I was one of them. But I sat with my new division, feeling displaced while my old team members would occasionally and uncomfortably glance across the room at me. Every member of the new team received an award that evening, including the MFH, while I sat alone, politely applauded, and held back tears of frustration while they accepted their awards amid whoops and hollers from their colleagues.

Despite the year's turmoil, my 2012 sales performance had been outstanding, but I was not rewarded. In essence, I was invited to the feast but not allowed to eat. Isolation and humiliation are powerful tools in the corporate retaliation playbook.

The attacks continued at that meeting. I was unprepared for the onslaught. Following a semi-lighthearted "contest" (pharma companies present everything as a contest to motivate salespeople), reviewing product information, the MFH pulled me aside and admonished me for winning.

"You're the smartest person I know, but why do you have to be so competitive?" he shouted at me.

I stared at him in disbelief—not that I was *not* the smartest person he knew (that was probably true). But didn't all sales managers want their employees to be competitive? I had no answer for his asinine comment and knew that whatever I said would be used against me. I kept my mouth shut, turned, and walked away with a slow, deliberate pace, but only at first. Once out of his sight, my walk became almost a run as I desperately tried to create distance between us. I can still feel the rush of rage and the heat of my flushed face as I practically marched back to my hotel room, muttering to myself, "You will not get away with this. You will not get away with this."

That was the bleak moment that broke me: a taste of their early smear campaign. It became a powerful inflection point—the exact moment in time that I decided to become a whistleblower.

I didn't know how to fight this battle or how long it would last, but this was about more than me. I would not become a victim, nor would I allow the company to make victims out of anyone else. I was wholly committed to the truth, stopping the illegal marketing of Gralise, and putting an end to the dirty money and dumping of pain medications into communities across the country.

Corporate America had the ability and resources to silence me, but their fatal miscalculation was underestimating the fire that burned inside me. To engage in this battle, I had to do it with a leopard's silent, stealthy precision and powerful attack. The hunted would now become the hunter.

I knew the retaliation would intensify, but I suddenly felt strengthened through grace and determination. Philip Yancey, a prolific American author, once observed that "grace, like water, flows to the lowest places," and I was in a very low place. With this sacred infusion, I was freed from fear and accepted that harsh times were ahead of me. The actions and words that were meant to destroy me would only strengthen my resolve. And with that emboldened attitude, I set out on my final stage as a Depomed employee.

Following the sales meeting, I was first up on the MFH schedule, a way to reinforce his power over me. Early the first morning, after driving three hours into my realigned territory, my further humiliation was his first order of business.

"Why are you doing this job?" he asked.

"Because I have a family to support, and I'm good at it," I replied, surprised by his bluntness.

"You should be looking for another job. Are you looking for another job?" he continued.

"No, I'm not, and why would you ask me that?" I decided it was best to switch from defense to offense.

Relentlessly, he continued, "I don't know why you're in this job."

I thought that maybe honesty was the best policy. "This is not the job that I was hired for. I would never have accepted a job where I had to drive three hours to get into the territory. This is what the situation is now, and I'm trying to make the best of it."

The bastard continued and repeated that I should be looking for another job. The verbal assault lasted throughout the day and into the next.

MFH saved his most offensive behavior for the car as we drove from office to office on a field ride. Shielded from public scrutiny, he let his true personality shine. His attacks became louder and more vicious. Yelling and berating me with accusations flying, I was a verbal punching bag. After hours of abuse, I tuned out. Strangely, the more he pushed, the calmer I became. My only response was to announce that he spoke very quickly when he was angry. That nonsensical but calculated response drew more ire, which continued until he stepped out of the car and into a physician's office. He was a veritable Dr. Jekyll and Mr. Hyde.

The field ride report written by this psychopath mirrored his view of the day, but not mine. He was laying a paper trail of my "poor performance," and I was laying an equally damning trail of his "unhinged performance." As long as I could make him feel that he held the upper hand, I could gather more evidence while withstanding his abuse. Like the leopard, my moves had to be calculated and unexpected.

Gaslighting came in the form of weekly calls. MFH continued to berate me on my poor sales performance. Predictably, as the gaslighting progressed, I began to believe him and stopped looking at the data. When I worked up the courage to take a look at how I stacked up against my peers, I noticed that I was holding steady in the top half of the group, not at the bottom as he repeatedly told me week after week. Remedial sales training was next on his list of tactics. As I went from award-winning representative to required viewing of "Sales 101" DVDs, the humiliation continued. The videos took me back to first grade, where the "dumb" label was applied because I couldn't see the board. Five decades later, the same label was attached to me for what I could see—the fraud and the lies that Depomed was trying to cover up. The unwatched videos went straight into the trash.

I knew I was biding my time at Depomed, so I kept a low profile, with one exception. The daily five-to-six-hour commute had aggravated sciatica in my right leg, with pain so intense I limped most days. I sought medical help and was advised to take gabapentin three times daily (ironic!) and get out of the car every 20 minutes for a brief walk. Upon leaving the doctor's office, I sat in the car and cried out of frustration and pain. The doctor had essentially written me out of my job unless I groveled and requested accommodations from management that was hell-bent on getting rid of me. So, I buried my pride and requested a minor accommodation. The answer was a swift and decisive no. This, too, was confirmation of Depomed's retaliation, and I assumed it would be incorporated into the legal complaint—a clear-cut violation of the Americans with Disabilities Act.

But the stress was taking a toll on my physical and mental health. Depomed management continued their daily and weekly assaults. I survived one last field ride with MFH and waited for another poor performance report. This one was exponentially worse than the last, littered with outrageous lies and painting me as completely inept. I took the opportunity to respond to their accusations in great detail, accusing them of inappropriate conduct with specific examples to back up my claims. Three pages later, that written response became my resignation letter and the basis for my future retaliation claim of constructive discharge: "involuntary resignation due to an intolerable work environment created by the employer."

Canary

Hopeful at first
Lighter than air
It seeps in
Silently suffocating.

Odorless, colorless
My lungs are heavy
Toxic poison
Escape NOW!

Immoral, unethical
Illegal, deadly
My soul is dying
Set me free
I have to warn the others.

(June 14, 2013, last day at Depomed)

CHAPTER 6

Blackberry Patch

*"Permanence, perseverance,
and persistence in spite of all obstacles,
discouragements and impossibilities:
It is this that in all things distinguishes the
strong soul from the weak."*
—Thomas Carlyle

By the age of four, I was on my own. Not literally, but it felt that way. My mother was occupied with my newborn sister; my brother, who was six years older, was excelling in school; and my dad was off to his daily job as an engineer at DuPont. I would dress myself in a hodgepodge of clothes and walk the one-third mile to the end of the block with my trusty dog, Sammy. We'd sit together in the blackberry patch while I told him stories and watched the world go by. I was content to sit quietly among the berries, brambles, and bees while I honed my observation skills and the ability to make myself invisible. Occasionally, when things didn't go my way at home, I would venture further, taking my stroller and baby dolls, and walk the entire block by myself, past the blackberry patch, past the smelly ginkgo tree, and around the corner to our neighbor's house. My dad would eventually come looking for me in the family station wagon and convince me it was time to come home.

I learned to take care of myself at a very young age with wisdom far beyond my four years on this earth. I understood that nature is solace; being alone is okay as long as your dog is beside you; and a walk is good for the soul.

Taking charge of situations was part of my early personality development and has remained with me throughout my life. My father frequently told me that from the time I could talk, my favorite phrase was, "I can do it myself." First grade, however, was a rude awakening. I didn't know how to read or write and had very little knowledge of the alphabet. All those hours spent in the blackberry patch had served my wild, creative side, but not my academic development. Sister Donna Marie, an imposing figure in her full black habit, often corrected me for my poor behavior, lack of attention, and even how I held my crayons. Very quickly, I was relegated to the remedial reading group and the label of "dumb" that came with it.

To correct this critical deficit, my mother scrambled to get me up to speed. She taped large alphabet letters to the fireplace mantel in the den, and every night she'd grill me by pointing at the letters with a yardstick. My job was to identify the letter and the sound. I remember it as a torturous way to learn, and the feeling of dread those lessons evoked crept into every aspect of school.

On February 14, 1968, I was fitted with my first pair of glasses while the other second-grade children exchanged Valentine's Day cards. Embarrassed and relieved at the same time, I now knew that the strange lights I'd seen at weekly mass were candles on the altar.

Things were finally falling into place. I knew my letters, how to read and write, and I could see. In my own mind, the "dumb" label didn't apply anymore, and I began to flourish, at least academically.

You don't make many human friends sitting in a blackberry patch, but as my reading skills increased, I found my soulmate. At eight, I discovered a companion who agreed with my penchant for blackberry patch adventures, talking with the animals, dislike of school, and disdain for bullies—Pippi Longstocking. Created by Swedish author Astrid Lindgren, Pippi and I had a lot in common. She was a nine-year-old girl with a freckled face, red pigtails, and mismatched socks. She lived alone with her animals and had a strong sense of justice, especially regarding animals. Self-sufficient, independent, quick-witted, and generous, Pippi would never let anyone shake her self-confidence, not even the bullies. Oh, there were so many things I loved about Pippi. I was painfully shy and wanted to adopt her boldness, especially regarding bullies.

With red hair, freckles, thick glasses, and a funny name, I provided plenty of fodder for the school bus ruffians. They seemed to truly enjoy humiliating me. Every day when I got off the bus, the mean boys would hang out of the windows, half-yelling, half-singing "The First Noel." Escape was the only way I knew to manage their cruelty. I'd run up the driveway as fast as I could to silence the taunting. I was determined to never let them see me cry. To my despair, my mother, with her usual lack of empathy and abundance of indifference, told me to get over it. Another early lesson in self-reliance.

Thanks to these early and formative childhood experiences, I learned many extraordinary life lessons. Today, I can see how they influenced the future me. The blackberry patch wisdom of a four-year-old and the Pippi Longstocking lessons as a young girl became the foundations of an intelligent, resilient, and underestimated woman in the corporate world.

For many years, I felt the stigma of underestimation, reminding me of the nuns who constantly scolded me for not being able to read or properly write my name. My resulting quiet personality contributed to the stigma. I always felt the need to prove myself not only competent, but better, much better, to dispel any notion that I could not achieve a specified goal. Along my journey, I have discovered the secret that puts underestimation in its rightful place—perseverance.

The next phase in my life as a whistleblower required immense perseverance, help, and direction. I had no idea where to begin, but I did have grit and determination. I called our family lawyer, who suggested another lawyer, who led me to another and then another. No one seemed to grasp the legal aspect of what I was trying to accomplish. I interviewed lawyers by telephone and in person. I found some through suggestions from friends. Exactly one year and one month after my resignation, I felt as though I had exhausted all avenues but was still no closer to finding the help I needed. The documents I had so carefully gathered and organized sat in a pile on the corner of my desk. They'd end up at the bottom of the to-do stack and, over time, recirculate to the top. Every time I saw the stack, I felt like a failure. I had accomplished part of my goal, but the mission was languishing as the ink on the papers was fading.

"Maybe this isn't going to pan out," I thought. "No one seems to care now, and certainly no one cared enough a year ago to join me. What an idiot I've been."

With a sweep of my arm, the stack of papers hit the metal trash can with a loud thud. For a long time, I stared down at the bundle of sales plans, projections, and scrap paper scribbled with incriminating conversations, now in disarray and crumpled. I had literally thrown my 25-plus-year career into the dumpster.

Emotionally spent but determined to move on from the Depomed disaster, I scoured online job postings every day. It was in July of 2014 when I discovered that job posting for a Pharma Fraud Consultant. I applied immediately, and the job poster responded with lightning speed.

When he called, one of his first questions was, "Have you ever seen fraud in the pharmaceutical industry?"

I almost laughed out loud. As I stared into the unemptied trash can still overflowing with two years' worth of documents, a smile came over my face. "Yes. I'm looking at the evidence right now!"

And with that one phone call, my truth-telling mission was back on track.

The first lawyer I met at Panera, the lawyer who looked straight out of *L.A. Law*, and not my potential abductor, confirmed that I had sound documents and a legitimate complaint and was not merely a disgruntled employee seeking revenge. A week later, I met with two lawyers to sign contracts and begin the process of transcribing my story. Sitting in a hotel room with them was initially awkward, but as I related my story, the words began to flow. For three hours, one lawyer asked questions while another took notes. Cautious about every answer I gave, one lawyer sensed my hesitation and questioned me about it. I assured him that I was completely forthcoming but didn't want any incorrect information associated with my name. One week later, lawyer number three emailed me a rough draft of the complaint.

By now, it was mid-September, and the lawyers and I had spent many hours going through the draft complaint line by line, word by word. If there was the slightest hint of inconsistency, I corrected it, much to the lawyers' surprise and frustration. Once we all agreed on the validity of the content, they carried out the final edits and filed the federal complaint in the jurisdiction of Washington, D.C., on October 30, 2014.

Relieved that I had come so far and found lawyers to help me, the truest test of my perseverance was just beginning. For the next decade, I managed the effects of corporate retaliation while drowning in the long, drawn-out process of legal action.

Initially, I thought that by raising my concerns internally, some corrective action would be taken. Of course, action was taken, but it was not to alter the course of the problem, but rather to change my course within the company through a demoralizing, never-ending campaign of retaliation, which is universally recognized as the most damaging consequence of whistleblowing.

Make no mistake, this was not simply my own misfortune, nor was it spontaneous. This was the corporate retaliation playbook. The moment I reported misconduct internally, I ceased to be an employee and became a liability. The company's objective was unambiguous: discredit me to protect the brand, the profit stream, and the individuals responsible for the unlawful conduct.

Retaliation is an engineered, deliberate, and coordinated operation designed to break the truth-teller. To be successful, the credibility, stability, and spirit of the whistleblower must be crushed. Retaliation functioned as a powerful weapon within Depomed. Later, I came to understand that I was not unique and that there is a recognizable and predictable pattern to silence all whistleblowers regardless of industry:

- Isolation – The predictable "change in territory" disguised as restructuring. Professional isolation became standard practice.
- Gaslighting – Reframing events to question my memory and credibility.
- Constructive interference – Creating conditions engineered for failure.

- Malicious use of managerial discretion – Workplace policies were weaponized against me under the guise of "performance issues."
- Blacklisting – Direct and indirect communication across the industry, ensuring that I was unemployable.
- Reputational demolition – Informal campaigns were designed to contaminate my professional identity.
- Constructive discharge – The predictable endpoint of my employment was when there was no possibility of satisfactorily performing my job duties.
- Personal intimidation – Threats were made to my physical safety with a clear warning message.

Once blacklisted, retaliation metastasized into my personal life. I was isolated and financially depleted. Career opportunities evaporated as I struggled to pay my bills; healthcare was too costly, so I went without it for almost 10 years. A three-decade professional identity was erased as if it had never existed.

The most unexpected bitter pill, however, was the legal process itself, which became a secondary mechanism of retaliation. Prolonged litigation, stretching more than a decade, functioned as a slow, sanctioned death. Depomed, with seemingly unlimited resources, weaponized procedural delays, confidentiality restrictions, and asymmetries of power. I was bound to legal silence. Meanwhile, Depomed continued operating and making profits, unhindered.

Legal safeguards exist to protect the whistleblower, but once the corporate wheels of retaliation were in motion, my life spiraled like bathwater down the drain. Had I not been well-versed in the art of perseverance and self-reliance early in my life, that might have been the end of my story. But I was still in the infancy of litigation against Depomed, and I, like Pippi, had no intention of letting the bullies force me into submission.

Gradual Warrior

Becoming a warrior is gradual
It does not happen in one apocalyptic event
You are transformed bit by bit
Until the day you have no choice
But to be a warrior.

The process is slow, intentional and quiet.
The journey begins with empathy
And recognition of courage
Cultured one person at a time
One story at a time.

And now it is in your blood-
Lying dormant mostly
It is a part of you.

Until the day
You speak up
You defy an injustice
You stand up for another who is suffering.

Practiced over and over
You have become.
There is no turning back now.
I am a warrior.

(October 2014, first complaint filed)

CHAPTER 7

Nuts & Bolts

*"And action is the only remedy to
indifference,
the most insidious danger of all."*
—Elie Wiesel

Here's the truth: I never wanted to be a whistleblower. I didn't wake up and decide that it was a good day to create total havoc in my life. It was not on my bucket list. In fact, being a whistleblower has taken away the opportunity to experience many of my bucket list items. Every other whistleblower I have had the privilege to speak with has expressed the same reaction—this was not part of our grand plan. The primary motivation of most whistleblowers is to expose unethical behavior, not to benefit financially.

So why did I, and other truth-tellers, take this road less traveled? The decision was a conscious, well-thought-out, albeit painful, process. There was nothing impulsive about it. Like other whistleblowers, I found myself face-to-face with a moral dilemma that I could not ignore. Indifference was not an option; silent complicity was not an option; and active complicity was out of the question.

Once I made the decision to act, I knew that I would almost certainly face the process alone. And I was correct. The psychological phenomenon known as the "bystander effect" gave me a glimpse into why my colleagues essentially abandoned me and, in essence, let me take the fall. The bystander effect is a social occurrence where people are less likely to help a victim when others are present, a concept explained by diffusion of responsibility (feeling less accountable) and group dismissal (assuming it's not an emergency if no one else reacts), leading to inaction in situations like bullying or accidents. In other words, even though hundreds of employees witnessed the same fraud, no one felt the need to address it because no one else was addressing it! How's that for circular reasoning?

For years, I couldn't explain why I felt so compelled to take action, incapable of walking away and carrying on with my life as all my colleagues had done. Maybe it was my Christian upbringing, or my anti-bullying, rebellious Pippi Longstocking nature, or the courageous family heroes I admired, or maybe it was the fact that I was a more mature and confident employee who was not easily bamboozled. In the end, there was no single reason why I chose to act, but a combination of all of those personality facets, aided and abetted by my anterior cingulate gyrus.

What? I know—no one (normal) has ever heard of this—but let me explain: the anterior cingulate gyrus (ACG), a critical structure deep within the brain's limbic system, plays a vital role in the complex process of whistleblowing. Acting as a central hub for integrating information, it helps signal the presence of an ethical dilemma, evaluates the potential costs and benefits of speaking out, and integrates social information and emotional responses into the final decision. The "whistleblowing mind" can be seen as a state where the ACG is highly engaged in navigating an intense moral conflict.

Individuals who blow the whistle exhibit strong ACG activation when faced with the opportunity for "dishonest gain," in contrast to individuals with psychopathic traits who show reduced ACG activity and less conflict during dishonest decision-making. The ultimate act of whistleblowing is a form of adaptive, highly challenging behavior that results from the ACG's processing of complex social, emotional, and moral information to guide a strategic, ethical decision.

So, my feeling of being compelled to act was an accurate description. Along with my previous life experiences and an overactive ACG, there was zero chance that I could encounter Depomed's alleged illegal marketing and look away. I had to face it head-on because people's health and lives were at risk.

Even though I felt alone when I brought this case to the Department of Justice in 2014, hundreds of citizens before me had faced the same dilemma. Whistleblowing, in the modern context, dates back hundreds of years and boils down to one essential act: an employee bringing to light illegal activity committed by their employer. The case hinges solely on the employee–employer relationship. Some who have heard my story believe I am condemning physicians or even patients. This is not the case. Physicians have the ability to prescribe as they wish within accepted standards of care. They face repercussions, though, if they accept bribes or kickbacks from anyone, including pharmaceutical companies, to alter their prescribing habits. Similarly, patients are free to take medication as they like and only occasionally encounter the long arm of the law when they abuse, sell, or trade prescriptions.

My first whistleblower lawsuit was filed under the *qui tam* provision of the False Claims Act. The term *qui tam* is shorthand for a Latin phrase, *qui tam pro domino rege quam pro se ispo in hac parte sequitur*, based in English common law, which means, "He who sues in this matter for the king as well as for himself." This centuries-old legal concept allows private individuals, often whistleblowers, to act as relators in exposing fraud against the government by filing a False Claims Act lawsuit. Passed during the American Civil War, the False Claims Act was designed to combat fraud by unscrupulous suppliers to the government. It empowers private citizens, typically insiders with knowledge of the fraud, to bring lawsuits on behalf of the government when they have reason to believe that a person or company has defrauded it. The relator's role is to initiate the legal process and remain in the process as a plaintiff by providing critical inside information otherwise unknown to the general public.

You may wonder why it was necessary to include the government in a case that involved me and my employer. The simplest explanation is this: the United States government, primarily through Medicare, Medicaid, CHIP, and military programs (VA/TRICARE), acts as the largest single payer and purchaser of healthcare services, funding nearly half or more of national health expenditures, making it the dominant third-party payer in the American system. When a pharmaceutical company encourages a physician to write prescriptions outside of the package insert (off-label marketing), they are directly engaging in fraud by causing a "false claim" to be submitted for reimbursement, especially pertinent if the patient holds insurance financed by the U.S. federal government with *your* tax dollars. While you may not have had any direct exposure to Depomed's supposed illegal marketing, every single American should be outraged that pharmaceutical companies routinely stuff their coffers by submitting false claims to the government, directly contributing to the national debt and, in my case, the opioid epidemic.

That's a heavy topic itself and offers a brief glimpse into why a specialized whistleblower attorney is necessary to expose the illegal activity and guide a process that tests the true will of those seeking to make wrongs right. The complex process is determined by federal and state statutes, with strict deadlines and hearings to hold the employer accountable for their wrongdoing. One misstep and the litigation falls apart. Unfortunately, I would bear the full weight of a misstep as the case concluded many years down the road.

The case against my employer was filed on October 30, 2014, under seal and *in camera*, in the District Court of Washington, D.C. My legal title was now a "relator." As mentioned above, a relator is a specific type of whistleblower who is involved in a legal action, acting as a plaintiff and suing on behalf of the government. In legal terms, "under seal" means a document is kept confidential, hidden from public view, to protect sensitive information, while *in camera* (Latin for "in chambers") refers to court proceedings happening in the judge's private chambers. Both concepts are designed to ensure the relator's privacy and the confidential nature of the claim while the government investigates it.

In practical terms, this meant that I was legally bound to silence for the duration of the case. The only people with whom I could discuss the details were my cadre of lawyers. Within a very short period, I was summoned to the obligatory high-stakes and high-anxiety relator meeting.

The closest analogy I can think of to a relator meeting is the Spanish Inquisition (investigations, secret proceedings, trials, and severe penalties). While it's an opportunity for a relator to bring their complaint to the government and make their case, the serious nature and people involved made me feel like I was the one on trial for heresy. And, in a sense, I was. The relator interview was not an adversarial setting, but not necessarily friendly either. My lawyers informed me that government agents would be watching my reactions and responses to their questions to gauge how reliable my information was and how I held up under pressure.

I had complete confidence in my evidence, but the anticipation was torturous. The walk from our hotel to the Department of Justice on the day of the meeting added to my anxiety. My lawyers barreled ahead as I tried to navigate the icy streets of Washington, D.C., in January. As I lagged behind, I wondered if they would even notice if I were kidnapped or if the evidence were stolen on the way to the meeting.

"Get a grip," I kept repeating to myself. "You've come this far. You can do this."

Once inside the imposing Department of Justice building, the layers of security added to my sense of doom: metal barricades, scanners, secure elevators, check-in points. Finally arriving at the room where the interview was to take place, I was taken aback by the austerity of it all: twelve cafeteria tables pushed together with a phone bank in the middle. No fewer than 15 government officials awaited my testimony. The room was filled to capacity, with all eyes on me. I awkwardly said hello and shook a few hands as they introduced themselves. I remembered no names, but the officials came from the FBI, DOJ, HHS-OIG, and DEA, and the phone bank was connected to attorneys general across the United States.

"Holy shit," I thought to myself, words that were not normally part of my vocabulary, but the intensity of the situation was settling in. I felt my heart race and, along with that, an inexplicable urge to run. I turned around so no one could see my face, because I knew I was being evaluated from the moment I walked through the door. One of my lawyers noticed and asked if I was okay.

"No, I'm not!" I responded quietly. Then I excused myself and headed for the restroom, fully aware that I was probably being recorded there, too. I began to wonder if this was what a panic attack felt like. Never had I experienced this surge of emotional and physiological onslaught. Once again, I repeated my mantra, "Get a grip. You've come this far. You can do this." I walked back into the room as confidently as I could and faced the music, so to speak.

The first statement from the United States Assistant Attorney General caught me off guard.

"Don't lie to us."

How absurd! *Why would I do that after everything I've endured to be sitting here with you?*

The questioning began with one agent and then moved to another and another. Once I started talking and presenting my evidence, my anxiety disappeared, and I began to feel more confident. After three and a half hours of grilling, my relator role was essentially complete. I had witnessed fraud, gathered evidence, and presented my case to the government. It was now in their hands, and very little was required of me while the government began its investigation to decide if the case had merit.

That was January 2015, and the case would drag on for another two years with only an occasional set of questions requiring my input. As I accepted the ritual of waiting, I thought about the case every day, optimistically hoping for the best. I certainly never thought something nefarious would come of it, until one day it did. My name was somehow revealed in the whistleblower case, and a few days later, as I was driving home from my husband's business during afternoon rush hour traffic, I was forced into the Jersey barrier by a large black SUV with tinted windows. I said a few choice words under my breath and then continued on my way home, almost forgetting about the incident—until it happened again two days later: same car, same location, same time of day. It was too eerie to just be a coincidence. This was no accident or poor driving. It was a deliberate attempt to intimidate and threaten me for speaking out.

When I told my lawyer about the incident, he informed me that the defendant's law firm was known for its dirty tricks. When I pressed him for more details, he suggested that I get a remote car starter installed.

"That would be great, especially in the cold weather," I responded.

His long silence gave me time to connect the dots.

"Are you talking about explosives being planted on my car?" I could hardly believe what I had just said. The thought of a Karen Silkwood demise startled me into the reality of the possible lethal consequences of my actions.

"It's not out of the question," he quietly said.

From that day on, and for years afterwards, I looked under my car before I started it each morning. I didn't even know what to look for other than something unusual or out of place. I replaced the naïve thought that "it couldn't happen to me" with hypervigilance. I changed the way I drove, how I put gas in my car, and where I shopped for groceries to avoid predictable patterns. Most notably, I was aware of people who were near me, as I scanned faces like an FBI agent. I avoided crowds and events and always had an exit plan mapped out in my head in public spaces. My world became smaller as I feared for my own and my family's personal safety.

By January 2017, the government voluntarily dismissed our case "without prejudice," meaning they did not want to pursue the allegations, but with the caveat that I could refile a case later if I wished. I was crushed. I felt that my time, effort, and sincere desire to hold Depomed accountable for their alleged fraud had been utterly wasted. While I desperately wanted to continue, my lawyers advised against it. My extreme disappointment in the government's conclusion soon became internalized, and I blamed myself for their dismissal of the case. Thoughts of inadequacy and failure were beginning to consume me.

This was a bleak period for me and my family. The financial repercussions of blacklisting were coming to fruition, and my personal life was taking a beating. Without a steady, adequate paycheck, we were forced to sell our home and move to a smaller house in a rural area where the cost of living was more in line with our now severely frugal budget. Homelessness was something that crossed my mind frequently. But that was far from the worst of it. We had recently discovered that one of my children was suffering from opioid addiction.

Every parent's almost-worst nightmare gutted me. When I realized what was going on, anguish erupted from me like lava gushing from a hot volcano. I crumpled to my knees with a grief-filled moan. I yelled out to God, "Why? How can this be? Have I not done enough to face down the devil?" If mine were a David and Goliath story, David was losing, and Goliath had the upper hand. It wasn't supposed to be this way. I had no tools to fight this battle and nowhere to turn. By the grace of God and the help of my sister and brother, our family began the long, long road of recovery that so many families have had to navigate. I am forever grateful to my siblings for stepping in when I needed it the most.

The inadequacies that I wrestled with over the dismissal of the whistleblower case became magnified in the wake of the destruction caused by addiction. Not only had I failed at the litigation process, but I felt that I had now also failed as a mother in the most essential task—to protect my child, a role dearer to my heart than any other. I was filled with anger at my child, anger at myself, and rage at the collective pharmaceutical industry. The news reported daily on the toll of the opioid epidemic, telling yet another tragic story of a family burying their child. There were days and even weeks when I had no idea where my child was or if they were alive or dead. I attempted to help, but everything I did was met with indifference, resistance, or hatred. Prayer was only mildly comforting because, in my mind, I received no direction and no answers. Mercifully, one cold night, I received a text from my child that they were ready to accept help. I had no idea what the road ahead looked like, but it was a tiny glimmer of hope.

Ultimately, the choice to accept help was my child's. The future was theirs to determine, but I had to take a long, hard look at my own actions that were not helpful to my child or our relationship. For me, it began with education. I attended seminars and meetings, and joined community and professional groups, looking for advice, answers, and healing. The most significant breakthrough for me came when I accepted that addiction was a brain-altering, life-taking disease that could only be countered with professional support, compassion, and knowledge. My child was willing to fight for themselves, and I was there to support the long road back to wellness. For those of you reading these words and facing the same struggle, please continue your fight. Recovery is not guaranteed, but it is possible.

The first steps of a fragile recovery for my child were now in place, but I could barely function. Chronic stress, anxiety, and hypervigilance from the lawsuit and then the anguish of my child's addiction, left my health suffering. I felt physically, emotionally, and morally depleted.

Then, an unexpected call from my lawyer in the summer of 2017, six months after the prior case's dismissal, gave me the boost I needed to get back on track. The opioid crisis was affecting every community in our nation, and politicians had decided it was time to take action. During the height of the crisis in 2017, the government primarily focused on declaring it a public health emergency and increasing funding for state-level initiatives. Equally important, and more significant on the legal front, politicians recognized the value in implementing measures to curb both overprescription and the flow of illicit drugs.

"Are you ready to take this on again?" my lawyer optimistically asked me.

With my rage toward pharmaceutical companies still fresh in my mind, and bearing the raw scars of the suffering of my child, my family, and countless other families, I practically shouted, "Hell yes!" into the phone.

Now that I was personally and professionally battle-tested, I was ready to take another stab at Depomed's alleged illegal marketing, and we began the entire process again. A fresh *qui tam* False Claims Act lawsuit with more robust evidence and a cadre of state co-plaintiffs to sign on was filed on October 30, 2017, ten months after the first suit was dismissed and four years after the first lawsuit was filed. This timeframe would later ring the death knell for settlement.

Truth Teller

"You're not a team player."
I'm a truth teller.
"No one likes you."
I'm a truth teller.

"You're making things difficult."
I'm a truth teller.

"You need remedial training."
I'm a truth teller.

"You will be relocated."
I'm a truth teller.

"This will teach you to keep your mouth shut."
I'm a truth teller.

"Good riddance."
I'm a truth teller.

"You're a liar."
I'm a truth teller.

"No one cares what you say."
I'm a truth teller.

"We did nothing wrong."
I'm a truth teller.

"We're not sorry."
I'm a truth teller.

"You deserve nothing."
I'm a truth teller.

"Guilty."
I'm a truth teller.

"You're a truth teller."
Yes I am.

(January 11, 2017, after first case dismissed)

CHAPTER 8

Melancholy

"We must be willing to let go of the life we planned so as to have the life that is waiting for us."
—Joseph Campbell

Why? Why? Why? Why would anyone put themselves through the process of bringing a whistleblower lawsuit when the odds are clearly stacked against them? The answer: whistleblowers are hard to silence. The truth-telling part of their brain seems to override the health and safety part, so they will endure all forms of retaliation for the sake of truth. This makes them dangerous to organizations engaging in fraud, and logically, that should make them extremely valuable to the government, but that is rarely the situation.

Despite the mountains of significant evidence that whistleblowers bring to the government, most cases and the truth-tellers themselves are dismissed. In 2015, Donald Soeken, America's best-known psychological counselor to whistleblowers, conducted a study concerning the fate of whistleblowers. The statistics are more than sobering: they're deeply discouraging. 90% of whistleblowers were fired or demoted; 27% faced lawsuits; 26% sought psychiatric or medical care; 25% became alcoholics; 17% lost their homes; 15% divorced; 10% attempted suicide; eight percent were bankrupted; less than five percent won their case. But an astonishingly high 84% said they would do it over again, although very few have had that chance.

I did have the opportunity to bring not one but two more *qui tam* False Claims Act complaints to the government. The most succinct answer as to why I would endure the laborious and exhausting process is simple—the mission was not yet completed. So strong was my conviction that Depomed needed to be held accountable for its alleged illegal marketing that I chose to sacrifice myself to that end.

In the spring of 2017, Missouri senator Claire McCaskill began an investigation targeting multiple opioid manufacturers, including Depomed, aimed at learning whether the companies had any role in the country's overutilization and overprescription of pain medications. The senator sent letters to the CEOs of the companies pressing them for answers and requesting internal documents concerning opioid abuse estimates, marketing strategies, sales quotas, and contributions to patient groups. Not surprisingly, the CEOs who had spearheaded the mass fraud against the American public were able to weasel their way out of any significant blame, other than a 2018 final report, which went largely unnoticed by the general public.

Strikingly, though, the 2018 U.S. Senate and Homeland Security & Governmental Affairs Committee report did expose the indisputable financial ties between opioid manufacturers and third party advocacy groups: "These groups have issued guidelines and policies minimizing the risk of opioid addiction and promoting opioids for chronic pain, lobbied to change laws directed at curbing opioid use, and argued against accountability for physicians and industry executives responsible for overprescription and misbranding." Between 2012-2017, Depomed was the third largest financial contributor to these lobbying groups, just behind Purdue and Insys, both of whom eventually faced severe financial penalties for their role in the opioid epidemic. Despite the revelation of this damning information, Depomed remained mysteriously unscathed.

In my mind, if you want to catch a thief in action, you don't ask the perpetrator of the crime for a list of their potential targets; you ask insiders who have the lowdown on what's going on. If any senator had really wanted the truth, they needed to look no further than the original 2014 *qui tam* false claims lawsuit that was dismissed a mere two months earlier by the Department of Justice. All the information was literally in plain sight and could have been accessed with a cursory glance in LexisNexis.

On behalf of the U.S. government, I filed a second completely new *qui tam* lawsuit in late 2017 and an amended complaint in 2018. Additional incriminating evidence was provided by a confidential witness who later became a secondary relator in the case against Depomed. These complaints revolved around two pain medications: Gralise and Lazanda. Lazanda was a transmucosal immediate release fentanyl (TIRF), a potent fentanyl nasal spray used to manage breakthrough cancer pain in patients who were already tolerant to around-the-clock opioid therapy. It was a very tightly controlled Schedule II substance due to its high potential for abuse, addiction, and overdose.

The exact same playbook that Depomed used to market Gralise was used to market Lazanda. The Department of Justice confirmed the playbook in their May 2025 press release. Once introduced in the market, sales representatives were directed to target pain specialists for conditions other than breakthrough cancer pain, such as general non-cancer pain, an unapproved and dangerous use. Depomed focused its marketing efforts on physicians who were already prescribing high volumes of similar fentanyl products, including some who had been flagged for diversion or were later indicted. The company placed high-volume prescribers on its speakers' bureaus and advisory boards, which constituted a form of kickback in exchange for prescribing Lazanda. Depomed developed a program allegedly designed to help ensure that Lazanda prescriptions, including those for off-label uses, would be approved by insurance providers like Medicare and TRICARE, leading to the submission of false claims to government healthcare programs for patients who did not meet the strict requirements for a Lazanda prescription.

If this sounds vaguely familiar, it is. Depomed had once again, in my opinion, negated all the protocols for ethical marketing, just as they had done with Gralise: off-label marketing to inappropriate physicians, highly incentivized pay for representatives who "performed," and kickbacks to high prescribers in the form of speaker fees. Lazanda, like Gralise, was a very effective pain medication for the correct patient, at the correct dosage, prescribed by an appropriate physician. But it appeared that Depomed's insatiable desire for market share and money ran so deep that they justified the fraud as a viable means to their end goal of profit, not patient benefit.

Essentially, Depomed adopted the Purdue-OxyContin playbook by targeting inappropriate physician specialties. While Depomed broadened the use of their drugs from one audience, general practitioners, to another, pain management, Purdue targeted general practitioners, who were not pain specialists. Patrick Radden Keefe's 2017 article, "The Family That Built an Empire of Pain," clearly lays out Purdue's marketing tactics, subsequently adopted by many companies marketing pain drugs. The effect was the same, though, a rapid and exponential rise in pain medication sales.

With the confidential, under-seal 2017 filing in November and an amended complaint in 2018, preparation began for two more relator meetings. Very similar to the first relator interview, these were high-stakes and high-anxiety affairs. The second meeting took place in San Francisco and the third in Washington, D.C. With hours of preparation and role-playing under my belt, I was becoming a confident and convincing plaintiff. The government now had two reliable relators, a plethora of evidence in complaints that would later be unsealed, and the names of Depomed management and higher-ups responsible for directing the unscrupulous marketing. There was talk of criminal charges being added to the civil charges of the existing lawsuits, which would have landed some of the most notable Depomed figureheads in jail.

Depomed, meanwhile, was taking steps to distance itself from its past. Carly Helfand, Executive Director of Fierce Pharma, hit the nail on the head when exposing the reason for Depomed's name change to Assertio Therapeutics in 2018. "The mounting litigation against Depomed plus investor scrutiny forced the company to do what many companies do when their reputations have been sullied by scandal and they need a solution to restore their good name: they change it ... Depomed no longer wanted anything to do with the opioid market, and clearly didn't want the public to remember its opioid phase either, considering the Senate probe in early 2017 that called the company's marketing practices into question."

Just to make certain all ties were cut with their old image, Depomed relocated its headquarters from California to Illinois and changed its product line. This attempt to distance themselves from their past did not absolve them from their previous fraudulent liabilities, and the Department of Justice investigation was only just beginning again.

As 2018 came to a close, the good ol' boy management at newly renamed Assertio Therapeutics was probably high-fiving its shiny new image and the fact that they still had not been forced to accept any significant responsibility for the suffering they had caused the American public. I, on the other hand, was sinking deeper into debt, despair, and isolation.

The dichotomy couldn't have been starker. The great hope I'd had after the third relator meeting faded, and there was no communication from the government. The case had reached a tipping point and hung in the balance like a high-rise crane on a windy day, swaying from side to side. Never knowing when it would all come crashing down, all I could do was wait. I bided my time in court-mandated silence as life slogged on for the next six years, longer than any other time period in this case.

With each new year, I hoped that the litigation would come to a successful end. Maybe 2019 was going to be the year. With continued silence, my focus shifted toward reflection on what my life was going to be like after litigation. I weighed different options and successfully completed a five-month paralegal course, but I was no closer to gainful employment than at the beginning of this saga. The paralegal avenue fizzled when the only question that my future employer cared about was how many words per minute I could type. Qualifications, education, and experience did not matter, but my ability in the typing pool was of utmost importance. With that as the sole criterion, I was once again searching for my true calling in life.

In my own estimation, I had failed at bringing a successful whistleblower suit, and in the process, had managed to destroy my 30-year career. I had failed as a mother, and now, without even beginning the role, I had failed as a future paralegal. That mountain of perceived failure obliterated my motivation.

Like tree branches exposed to the winter's chill, failure has a way of laying one's soul bare and vulnerable. Beautiful in one sense, but wholly uncomfortable in another. It was a desolate time, and I found true joy in very few things, with one exception: my dogs, my emotional anchors.

They were two delightful rescues who were very different creatures in personality, physical appearance, and age. Chloe, my senior golden retriever, was approaching her sixteenth birthday. Gifted to my daughter for her tenth birthday, in lieu of a horse, she was a family member through and through. Sadly, but predictably, time was stealing her from us every day, bit by bit. In February 2019, she walked more slowly but seemed to be in reasonably good health until one day she lay down and looked at me as if to say, "Tell me goodbye now. It won't be long." Family members filtered in, offering long hugs and whispering loving words of goodbye. For several days, she bravely continued her fight as I carried her out to her favorite tree, where we'd sit and soak up a few moments of warmth in the February sunshine. As vultures circled overhead, sensing her imminent death, I knew the time had come. Each evening, I would lie down beside her, gently stroking her silver-tinged golden fur. On February 5, as quiet music played in the background, she exhaled one final breath with a long, slow, ear-piercing, primal howl. I, too, moaned with a depth only known to grief. She was gone, taking a part of my soul with her.

Hers had been a wonderful life, full of family love and adventure, and she reciprocated with a sweet and always-tolerant spirit. With the reverence reserved for the most special souls, we buried her on our family property, gently placing her frail, cold body in a gravesite facing the sunrise. Her canine companion, Cooper, lay on top of her gravesite for weeks, sniffing the ground. He chose her dog bed over his own at night. No doubt, the depth of his sorrow equaled ours.

Her absence felt like a gaping wound. Words could not fully describe my sense of loss, but the bronze sculpture *Melancholy* by Hungarian sculptor Albert György portrayed the raw depth of my sadness. A bronze figure sitting on a bench slumped over, with a huge void in its chest, *Melancholy* symbolizes the immense emptiness and profound sorrow of grief, heartbreak, and deep emotional pain from losing a loved one.

As one observer noted, "For anyone who has ever felt the loneliness of 100 rooms, or the weariness when you've lost the battle; for anyone who is so bereft that they feel like an empty shell or to those who found themselves dissolving over the loss of something so precious; György is speaking to you, for he knows exactly how that feels."

Thank you, Albert György, for sharing your pain in such a universally powerful and profound way.

While still wrestling with grief, I knew I had to do something, anything, to quiet my rising despair. My personal strategy has always been volunteering. Giving back to the community while trying something new in a low-expectation environment was just what I needed. Combining my respect for veterans and my lifelong love of dogs, I began volunteering at an organization training service dogs for veterans with PTSD. The volunteer work became a psychological breakthrough for me because I was no longer dwelling on the whistleblower case or the profound loss of Chloe. Witnessing the healing bond between the veterans and their dogs was restorative for me as well.

I practiced my training skills on one dog in particular: Marcella, a young and independent-minded golden retriever. She had already been identified as a possible "career change" dog (one who would not complete service dog training), but in my eyes, she was perfect in every way, and I looked forward to my weekly interaction with her.

Several months into volunteering, I had to bow out briefly because my own companion dog, Cooper, was showing signs of illness. One week became two weeks and then three. I was now in the throes of multiple vet visits to determine the cause of his illness. The persistent cough, lethargy, and weight loss signaled something ominous. His illness progressed quickly, and within a month, he was diagnosed with dilated cardiomyopathy (DCM), a serious heart disease in which the heart muscle weakens, thins, and stretches, causing the chambers to dilate, making it difficult to effectively pump blood. This leads to poor circulation, heart failure, and fluid buildup in the lungs—essentially, the dog dies a painful death akin to drowning.

Cooper was a Great Dane–lab mix, and DCM is most common in large breeds like Great Danes, but can also be caused by infections, genetic mutations, or nutritionally induced, with a strong correlation to grain-free dog food. I had been feeding Cooper grain-free food for years. Tragically, I believed the nonsense pushed by dog food companies, most of whom are divisions of big pharma companies, that it was the best way to feed your dog. Once the reality set in that I had rescued him as a puppy and now essentially killed him as an adult, I couldn't forgive myself.

In late May 2019, three and a half months after Chloe's death, Cooper passed away. But relief for him came through euthanasia, which meant I had to make the agonizing decision about the time and place. I held his now withering body in my lap and cradled his head as the vet did her solemn duty. Through my tears, I whispered to him how much I loved him and that he would soon see Chloe again.

"He's on his way now," the vet calmly said as she pushed the phenobarbital through his veins.

He put up a valiant fight, but of course, the lethal dose of anesthetic overtook his consciousness and any sensation of pain. He was out of his misery. My own misery and guilt multiplied tenfold that day. Buried next to Chloe, they are together again. I visit their graves daily and thank them for the wonderful dog life lessons they taught me—patience, tolerance, love, kindness, and forgiveness.

For the first time in decades, I was dogless, and it was a wretched feeling. Losing both of them in such a short period of time was traumatizing and confusing. I literally felt out of place in my own home and my own skin. If you have ever loved and lost a dog, you will understand the sadness, depression, and loneliness that replace that deep, unconditional bond. No matter how society views or dismisses the death of a pet, I felt the full weight of grief in losing another family member.

In the dog training world, this series of multiple stressful situations occurring one right after another is known as trigger stacking. The immediate emotional response in both dogs and humans is fight, flight, or freeze. I no longer had the energy to fight, nor to flee. I was frozen emotionally and physically. One final trigger during the summer of 2019 would almost bury me, but instead it became an inflection point, a time of contemplation, reflection, taking stock, and life-changing decisions.

Several weeks after Cooper's death, my father celebrated his 88th birthday with our usual family tradition. The kids, grandkids, and great-grands gathered at my sister's river house to enjoy each other's company and the serenity of the Rappahannock River. As we sat on the dock soaking up the afternoon sun, my dad started talking about recent dreams revolving around his time in active duty during the Korean War. Until that day, I had never once heard my father mention any war stories. But on this day, at this moment, he vividly recounted being tortured by enemy forces, describing the horror of the sights, sounds, and smells in intricate, minute detail. I was simultaneously horrified and engrossed by his descriptions. Unfortunately, neither my sister nor brother was close enough to hear his account, and out of respect for my father and the intensity of the stories, I didn't interrupt him or the flow of his narrative in order to bring my siblings in on this once-in-a-lifetime conversation.

For more than an hour, horrendous descriptions of abuse, confinement, and beatings spilled out of him as if they had been suppressed for many years. In fact, they *had* been for almost seven decades. Oh, how I wished my siblings could have heard and experienced what I did on that day. My later retelling of my father's stories to my brother and sister lacked the fire and brutality that he had shared with me. On that afternoon, I experienced the most surreal display of emotional turmoil that I had ever witnessed in my father.

For many weeks that summer, I tried to process the life-changing events that were swirling around me—the riveting revelations from my dad, the deaths of my two dogs, and the silence and isolation of litigation. Each was a burden that was slowly crushing me. The roller coaster ride of emotional turmoil welled up inside me, and I felt powerless to act. I was being swept into the riptide of grief and could not get my footing. I began to wonder if my family would be better off without me. After all, I had created the whistleblowing dilemma, and now my entire family was suffering in one way or another. One late summer afternoon, I sat alone in my office, head buried in my hands, tears streaming down my face, and I pleaded with God to give me direction or take me from this life.

The only explanation I have for what happened next is divine intervention. In that moment, sitting in my office, everything changed. My foggy mind cleared, and I knew precisely what I was going to do and how I would accomplish it. My father's revelations had strengthened the admiration and empathy I felt for our military heroes as they quietly carried the wounds of war for years and sometimes decades. Through my recent volunteer work, I have witnessed the restorative power of dogs for veterans with PTSD. I felt called to bring those experiences together and help others heal by training service dogs for veterans and those suffering from disabilities.

Within a month, I enrolled in the master's degree program at Bergin University of Canine Studies. My own personal renaissance was taking place, guided by faith and the seemingly unrelated traumas in my life. The tide was turning in a positive direction, but one final confirmation of my new path awaited me. On my 59th birthday, only days before the master's program at Bergin was to begin, I received the most marvelous surprise. Marcella, the golden retriever I had briefly helped train, had been returned to the organization by the veteran with whom she had been paired. She was gifted to me, and with an unbelievably grateful heart, I accepted. There was no doubt in my mind that I was being guided to this new vocation. In late August 2019, Marcella and I together began our new "leash" on life.

Land of Hypocrites

In the land of hypocrites
Everything is sunny
The world sparkles
With truth-blinding light.

All who enter must abide
By the unspoken rules
Look and recite
But do not pry beneath the surface.

Do not think, do not analyze
And above all, never question.
The sugar-coated leaders
In the land of hypocrites.

If you think
You will be shunned
Dismissed and alone.
Demonized, demoralized.

Harassed and humiliated
You will be driven out
Because you speak without illusion
Truth is forbidden in the land of hypocrites.

(January 23, 2024, almost 10 years into litigation)

CHAPTER 9

Most Precious Gift

*"The bond with a true dog is as lasting as the
ties of this earth will ever be."*
—Konrad Lorenz

The concept of divine intervention and "being called" is a tiny bit uncomfortable for this occasional Doubting Thomas. Maybe God meant to call someone else. Or maybe He didn't. Looking back over the course of events that led me to Marcella, the evidence is irrefutable—one cog out of place in my universal wheel, or hers, and the outcome would have been vastly different.

In the short 12 months since Marcella's birth, she had already been rejected multiple times: passed around like a big sister's hand-me-downs through two previous organizations and one owner. Before being gifted to me, her fourth owner, she had been transported from the west to the east coast, but I would be her forever person, and she would have her forever home. The intersection of our two lives, at just the moment we both needed each other, was nothing short of, dare I say, miraculous.

With the arrival of Marcella and a new career on the horizon, I began to reflect on my old life as I second-, third-, and fourth-guessed every decision I had made.

Working in the pharmaceutical industry, I had always felt a moral disconnect. While the industry's mission was altruistic, at least on the surface, the true mission was always profit, and fraud was rampant. It took me decades to release myself from that world because I genuinely wanted to believe I was helping patients. But, like Ebenezer Scrooge, forced to stand before his grave by the Ghost of Christmas Yet to Come, I feared that one day I would wake up to realize my pharmaceutical industry life had been shallow and vacant. I needed to find my own road to redemption and, like Ebenezer, grab on to my new life with both hands.

Marcella was my gift of redemption. She gave me new energy, purpose, and the strength to continue fighting the endless litigation against Depomed. Even her name represented the warrior that I needed to stand beside me. Marcella is the feminine form of Marcus/Mars, the Roman god of war. Not long after she entered my life, I added the name "Tullamore" to her AKC registration in honor of our family's Irish heritage. Tullamore (Tully) became a family member through and through, but I was her person.

Every dog has a person, and with love, not luck, that feeling is reciprocated. From the moment I was first introduced to Marcella/Tully, we bonded, even though I only interacted with her for an hour or so weekly, and then later not at all as Cooper fell ill. But we had a connection. Having had golden retrievers my entire adult life, I clearly formed a canine preference and naturally gravitated toward her. And of course, I had only recently lost my beloved Chloe, a golden mix, which undoubtedly influenced me. And why did she gravitate toward me? I think she could sense I needed comfort, love, and protection, and she had plenty to give.

The profound connection between dogs and humans has been recognized and celebrated for millennia. Theodorus Gaza, a fifteenth-century Greek humanist, beautifully highlighted the profound nature of dogs, emphasizing their loyalty, companionship, and role as beloved members of humanity. For many years, I have loved his well-known description in a 1460s letter accompanying the gift of a female puppy to a "most illustrious man":

The gift which I am sending you is called a dog, and is in fact the most precious and valuable possession of mankind.

Gaza presents the dog as a deliberate, precious gift, more valuable than all human creation. His description of a dog's selfless love, companionship, and unique bond with humans still rings as true today as it did in the fifteenth century.

But dogs have not always enjoyed such an elevated status. Their value rose and fell in civilizations according to the whims of society as David Grimm, a science journalist, masterfully recounts in his bestselling 2015 novel, *Citizen Canine*. From possessions of the wealthy to victims of unanesthetized vivisection, dogs have benefited from human companionship and borne the brunt of brutal human experimentation.

During my own life, I have witnessed the elevation of my dogs from outdoor, free-roaming pets to cherished family members, complete with their own array of accessories, rivaling those of a human toddler. I wince when I think of Sammy, my first dog, and how we fed and housed him (the vet's canned dog food and an outdoor doghouse) compared to the lives of my current canines: multiple orthopedic dog beds scattered about the house, homemade food and supplements, baskets of squeaky toys, and chew bones of all shapes and sizes.

The timeless idea that dogs enrich our lives immeasurably is a feeling shared by countless dog lovers across centuries, and the deaths of my two cherished companions brought this sharply into focus for me. As I told a friend shortly after their passing, "There are very few people in this world that I will mourn more than those two dogs." Even at the time, I was shocked by the vulnerability in that statement that embodied my grieving heart and mind trying to process their deaths, but more importantly, it was the deep-down truth.

In all its unfiltered rawness, it sparked a curiosity in me: How could I be so devastated by the deaths of my two dogs? Society clearly values humans more than animals, but what I had expressed out loud seemed to imply the opposite or, at the very least, that I valued my dogs on a par with human family members. Could I really be as, or possibly more, connected to my dogs than to people? I wondered why I felt such an emotional draw toward dogs, not just at this time, but my entire life. It was as if I were looking into a mirror and seeing the little girl sitting in a blackberry patch with her dog. My past and present were connected through a lifetime of dogs, but I couldn't quite put my finger on why or how that bond was so essential for me. To understand the four-year-old me, the adult I became, and the decisions I had made, I needed to understand the why and how of this human–canine bond.

When I enrolled at Bergin University of Canine Studies, this was the central burning question I wanted to answer. And apparently, others were asking the same thing. World-renowned scientists were investigating the fundamentals of this extraordinary bond. Clive Wynne, PhD, a professor of psychology at Arizona State University who studies the behavior of dogs, expressed my thoughts exactly: "Clearly, there's something remarkable and unique about how dogs live with people. What is the underlying process that makes this relationship so special? How do people and dogs fall in love with each other?"

Answering those questions and understanding the relationship between dogs and humans is at the heart of the growing field of dog cognition.

As I threw myself into the academic and research world of canine cognition, I could feel my spirit rebound. I devoured every morsel of information and was equally fascinated and humbled. How could I have lived with dogs my whole life and not known this information? The answer: We humans have only just begun to understand the complexity of the canine mind and the human–canine bond.

Our longest and truest companions, dogs have literally been walking beside us for the last 30,000 years, possibly longer. They were the first animals to be domesticated. Masters of observation, dogs understand human gestures and language to a greater degree than our closest primate relatives. Their senses, especially olfaction, are far more developed than ours, allowing them to view the world, relationships, and emotions through their superior and precise sense of smell.

Gregory Berns, MD, PhD, a professor of psychology and distinguished professor of neuroeconomics at Emory University, was the first researcher to peer inside the minds of dogs using functional magnetic resonance imaging (fMRI). His cutting-edge research, described in his 2013 book, *How Dogs Love Us,* and later in the *Journal of Medical Ethics* (2018), stated: "Advances in neuroscience imply that harmful experiments in dogs are unethical." His research ushered in a long-overdue model of ethical scientific research on dogs. On the practical side, his observations confirmed that dogs really do love us and not just our ability to provide them with food. Berns's revolutionary work revealed how dogs think and feel, how they choose which humans to cooperate with, and even what their memories are made of.

From all over the world, scientists contributed to the understanding of our universal best friend. Enikő Kubinyi, PhD, a professor and head of ethology at Eötvös Loránd University (ELTE) in Budapest, Hungary, is well-known for her groundbreaking research on dog behavior, cognition, and the unique dog–human bond. "Dogs are increasingly stepping into the human emotional and relational gap, not merely as pets, but as surrogate children or companions ... dog-human relationships combine the best of friend relationships and parent–child bonds, making them more supportive and positive than most relationships between humans." Dr. Kubinyi's research confirmed the validity of the intense, raw grief I had felt following the deaths of my dogs. Science is now putting hard data to what we dog lovers already knew.

And the very best news of all: Dogs share a deep, biological connection with humans, beyond behavior. They mirror human biology by syncing their heart rate, breathing, and hormones with us. When a dog and its owner are relaxed, their heart rate variability (HRV) align, a sign of shared emotional states. Conversely, when we're stressed, dogs detect our mood through volatile organic compounds in our breath and sweat. By subtly mimicking our emotional and arousal states, dogs create a feedback loop that reinforces our bond and helps calm us. The simple act of petting a dog or looking into its eyes triggers the release of oxytocin, known as the love hormone, in both humans and dogs, similar to parent–infant bonding.

So what does all this physiological and psychological mirroring between humans and dogs mean? It means we are, quite literally, tuned into each other. Biologically, emotionally, and behaviorally, dogs have the capacity to relate to humans in a way no other animal can. These wonderful nuggets of dog-ness are precisely the reason dogs make excellent companions and therapy animals. We are made for each other.

The little girl in the blackberry patch could feel every ounce of this exquisite relationship with her dog, Sammy.

With each dog that came after him, I cherished an equally profound bond. But it wasn't until six decades later that I realized the *necessity* of that relationship in my life. Sammy, Destin, Cecil, Leo, Chloe, and Cooper loved me exactly for who I was, no strings attached. I was not forgotten, dismissed, or rejected. I was not ashamed, embarrassed, or afraid when I was with my dogs. When I spoke to them, I didn't fear verbal or physical repercussions. I didn't need to run away, hide, or make myself invisible. They did not bully me or make me feel unworthy. I was never disowned or relegated to second choice in their eyes. On the contrary, when I was with them, I was fully accepted, loved, appreciated, and first choice: pure love, simple and uncomplicated, as the best things in life usually are. It was exactly what I needed. And it came from a dog.

I had felt the enormous capacity of a dog to love me, and now I was privy to the science behind how and why they love us. It was time to put my personal insight and newfound knowledge to use, beginning with Tully, the most precious gift. In the coming months, she would be my guide and mentor as I incorporated science and art into training service dogs.

But I had one last obligation before graduating and leaving Bergin. My colleagues nominated me as our class's commencement speaker. I was thrilled, although a bit suspicious as to whether I was actually nominated or simply the last person standing who had not refused the task. To the surprise of my skeptical heart, they really had chosen me!

The 15-minute talk overflowed with gratitude. I sincerely thanked each colleague and then spoke of our collective obligation to be of service to the dogs and people who needed us. We had reparations to pay, in the form of new knowledge, to the dogs who had suffered at the hands of humans who may or may not have known better. With all of the power vested in me (none actually), I sent my colleagues and myself out into the world to be dog disciples. To this day, I continue to share the message that communication, respect, and love, not obedience or submissiveness, are the true heart of the human–canine relationship and, quite frankly, every relationship.

Inquisition

Passes, gates, guards,
To floor 13
The unknown
Panic finds me.

So many faces
Staring, leering,
Waiting for confidentials
Blunders, fumbles, missteps.

My mind races.
I need to run.
I have to stay.
I should be used to this.

Panic settles
When the words flow.
I spill corporate secrets again
And return to silence
Again.

(September 2018, after third relator meeting)

CHAPTER 10

Betrayal, Bullies, and Belonging

"Life tried to crush her,
but only succeeded in creating a diamond."
—John Mark Green

As the years silently flowed, one into the other, I received no news concerning the whistleblower lawsuit. Dead silence. I feared the case was dead, too. As time passed, I knew the value of the suit was decreasing and wondered if there was anything left to be salvaged from it. Early in the process, I emailed the lawyers every month for an update. That timeline stretched to every quarter, and then only once a year. Discouraged and frustrated by the lack of information, I essentially stopped communicating with them for a time. This is not to say that I wasn't paying attention to other legal cases, news, or precedents being set, but it seemed I was the only one still interested. When one of the core lawyers in the case resigned and moved on to an entirely different area of practice, I took it as a sign to let go of any hope of resolution and accept defeat. But I couldn't do that—my middle name is perseverance.

As spring of 2021 approached, the world seemed (mostly) right. Although there was only silence on the legal front, my self-appointed dog discipleship was going well. Training clients and speaking engagements kept me from concentrating on the languishing whistleblower battle. My fledgling business, The Blue Paw Project, was named in honor of Cooper and his blue paw print that I had created on the day he crossed the rainbow bridge. The mission was to educate people about the importance of understanding canine communication.

Cooper had been a scaredy dog, afraid of absolutely everything. Fear had ruled his life and prevented him from truly flourishing. I had worked with him daily to build his confidence, and after nine years (!), he had finally come out of his shell. But by then it was too late—his health took a dramatic turn for the worse, and there was no more training, only easing of pain. As he lay dying in my arms, I made a promise to him that I would do everything I could to make sure no one ever gave up on their fearful dogs. This was the genesis of The Blue Paw Project, created in homage to Cooper.

During my tenure at Bergin, I was shocked and disappointed to realize that so many dog owners and professionals had very little understanding of how dogs communicate, putting their children, grandchildren, and themselves at risk for dog bites. This was an area where I could make a difference and possibly change the course of a tragic outcome for both the human and the dog. I spoke to audiences nationwide and internationally on the topic of canine body language, adding weight to the message with statistics on dog bites and subsequent dog relinquishment and euthanasia. Talking about these issues stirred some controversy, but controversy was better than indifference. Few people, however, were willing to accept the responsibility of preventing future tragedy. Most were fully, but mistakenly, confident that this tragedy could never happen to them.

This type of calamity can be prevented, but then there are some issues over which we have no control: the personal tragedy that hits like a lightning bolt and burns like a raging fire, a parent's-worst-nightmare tragedy. Once again, heartbreak struck our family, and in the cruelest way. My 36-year-old stepson, who had, against all odds, recovered from a traumatic brain injury a year earlier, was suddenly suffering from seizures. As he was no longer able to drive or work because of the unpredictable nature of his illness, his world had become smaller while waiting for his health to rebound.

And then, one summer afternoon, we received the tragic news that he had suffered another seizure, but this time the prognosis was grim. He was taken to a local hospital in grave condition. I urgently called family members who were spread out across the U.S. and who rushed to his bedside. The instant I laid eyes on him, I knew there was no overcoming this horror— sepsis had invaded every organ. His liver and kidneys had shut down, and his heart was weak. Kept alive by dialysis, an entire wall of medications, and too many IV lines to count, that haunting sight of our cherished son is seared into my mind.

We each took turns saying our goodbyes to this bright, funny, charming, and mischievous son, brother, and uncle. As I stroked his hair, I told him to watch over all of us when he got "home" because we would need to know his love was shining down on us. I kissed him on the forehead, knowing I would never see his impish grin or hear his distinctive laugh again. Several hours later, in the chaos of a hospital room filled with the brave nurses and doctors who tried to revive him, death snatched him from us suddenly and violently and took our souls, too. From that day on, our family would never be the same.

There is nothing in life that can prepare you for the loss of a child, no matter how old they are. The laws of nature are violated. Parents who bury their young hold silent, deep scars that will never heal for the rest of their lives. Siblings suffer and grieve a different kind of loss, distinct from parents' grief, and yet loss binds us together. Everything in our universe stopped to honor and grieve the young life taken exactly one month before his 37th birthday.

How dare the world carry on as if his life and death didn't matter!

I was angry at God, at Depomed, and at the Department of Justice, an unusual trio. While they may not seem related, they were, because the lawsuit had lingered so long that we were financially depleted. We couldn't afford to bury our own son. That was the ultimate gut punch. We had to ask for help to manage the costs of his funeral. In this darkest of times, I was afraid we would not survive.

The betrayal of the universe is the highest form of treachery. The deep pain of untimely death brings the fragility of life into sharper focus—a call for us to live boldly, and in the moment, because tomorrow is never guaranteed. Through death, everything falls away, exposing the raw truth of our own existence. Why did such a beautiful young soul have to suffer? If I could have taken his place, I would have. It should have been me. His death felt like the ultimate betrayal, and as the specter of unworthiness reared its ugly head again, I thought about betrayal in my own life.

How is it possible that I have no childhood memory of a hug or an "I love you"? Not one. Was I not worthy of a parent's love? Relegated to remedial in my early school days, did no one think to offer a helping hand instead of a label? I felt the emotional and physical betrayal when my mother repeatedly raised her hand against me. Was I not worthy of understanding, patience, or kindness? Corporate America betrayed me with its lies and gaslighting. In that instance, though, I was not the only one harmed. Patients and families were damaged irreparably in some cases. And that's why I could no longer allow the betrayal to continue.

My self-reflection continued, moving into the whistleblower lawsuit. What had gone wrong? Why was there still no resolution? Maybe I could have been a more convincing relator—maybe I should have recorded conversations instead of relying on handwritten notes. Would another lawyer have made a difference? Maybe I should never have taken a stand in the first place. What made me think I could take on the powerful and corrupt pharmaceutical industry? In the absence of information and an abundance of doubt, all the woulda-coulda-shoulda questions swirled around me.

In the fog of grieving our son's death, my own mind was beginning to betray me. Maybe I was the root cause of the operation going wrong. My logical brain knew that was not the case. I had spent over a year carefully analyzing, re-analyzing, and over-analyzing the situation at Depomed, and assessing the pros and cons of coming forward before I made any moves on the legal front. The scenario from beginning to end to beginning played out over and over in my mind.

Searching for answers, as whistleblowers caught in the long game of retaliation often do, I uncovered some universal truths about whistleblowers. Whistleblowing itself is a uniquely solitary activity, but as a group, whistleblowers share the same emotional triggers: betrayal, bullies, and belonging.

Almost every act of whistleblowing is the result of organizational, not individual, failure. To protect themselves, organizations flip the narrative by devaluing and labeling the whistleblowing employee as a snitch, emotionally unstable, or morally suspect. This betrayal deeply injures morally courageous whistleblowers and sets off a cascade of events. Most of us know it's coming, at least from management, but the betrayal of colleagues is unexpected and cuts even deeper. As former friends back away, careful not to be associated with us, we are left to stand alone, completely vulnerable to the wrath awaiting us.

Author Charles Alford sums it up perfectly in his 2015 article "What Makes Whistleblowers So Threatening?" He writes: "Everything you need to know about whistleblowing you learned in secondary school. Above all, how it feels to be left out of the group, excluded, rejected. What it is like to walk into the school cafeteria and be left to sit alone. What it is like to be mocked or bullied. This is the most feared retaliation of all, and most do not even know it. It is why we are so ambivalent about whistleblowers. Are they not really just whiners and malcontents? For if they are not, then the whistleblower reveals by contrast the cowardice of us all."

I felt the whistleblower's stigma before I officially blew the whistle because I always refused to go along to get along. I could not turn my eyes away from the corruption. It was not in my nature and never had been. The ability to separate myself from the organization was not a lack of something, but rather the addition of something. The sycophantic emperor's-new-clothes kind of organizational loyalty smacked of superficiality. My alternative and deeper loyalty was directed toward humanity, especially those who were suffering. Whistleblowers speak up to correct not only organizational wrongs, but injustices against their fellow humans, often rooted in injustices we've felt in our own lives.

Those perpetrating betrayal share the same mindset as schoolyard bullies, but with more power and control over a whistleblower's future. From the time I was a very small child, I had cultivated an intense disdain for bullies, but I was powerless to do anything about it. The only power of that little girl was to escape and become invisible. My sensitive soul longed for human love and attention, but survived on imagination and the unconditional love of my dog.

As an adult, though, not only did I have a degree of power, but I also had options and had developed a strong moral character, rooted deeply in empathy and responsibility. When I took a stand, I did it not only for myself, but also for those who felt powerless. Depomed became the biggest bully in the schoolyard when their true game plan, profit, was in jeopardy. I knew, and they knew, that I was a threat to the organization. This time, I would not hide; I would not become invisible; and I most definitely would not let the bully win.

One particularly telling bully incident during my Depomed employment involved a training session on how to present Gralise to physicians, framing its favorable managed care profile, which insurance companies would pay for off-label uses. While the other employees regurgitated the company line, I chose a different tactic.

"How many of you have ever had shingles?" I began. "How many of you know someone who has ever suffered from post-herpetic neuralgia?"

No one raised their hand, but I could feel an uncomfortable tension rising in the room. I continued, "The pain is unlike anything you've ever felt. If your parents or grandparents were suffering from PHN, would you allow them to suffer, or would you search out the most effective, safest pain relief possible? Chronic, unrelieved pain is a terrible burden and in the most extreme circumstances can lead to suicide."

And then I quietly returned to my seat. Not one word was spoken by anyone in the room. My message was clear, concise, and centered on the patient's suffering, not the bilking of insurance companies. It was also the truth, not a concept widely accepted in the pharma world. Later, a sales trainer approached me and tried to throw a barb my way.

"I just can't figure you out. That was not the point of the training session."

I just smiled and turned away. His disparagement of me was evidence of my success. It was a win. Easing suffering should be the goal of the healthcare industry, not the quickest route to the fastest buck. Each small win incrementally transformed me. The years of humiliation, betrayal, and self-doubt could have crushed me. Instead, I was now being forged by my brokenness. I was not born into it, but I was becoming a warrior armed with truth, courage, and empathy. What the bullies had torn down, I was rebuilding and restoring.

By now, you know I walked away from the pharmaceutical world with all of its trappings and lies. But I walked straight into nothingness: betrayed, bullied, and now blacklisted. I belonged nowhere. Isolation is a powerful psychological tool used against whistleblowers because it works, and it's a clear warning to others: "Do not cross this line or we will break you, too."

I had cut ties with my former career, and my colleagues had cut ties with me. I was sailing between continents with no land in sight. Like most whistleblowers, I felt profoundly alone, even abandoned at times, not an entirely new feeling for me. Lawsuits filed under seal require silence, and I was willing to pay the price to expose the corporate wrongdoing and create change. I just had no idea how long the silence would last, or if it would ever end.

During the seemingly never-ending legal battle, Tully was my living, breathing antidote to betrayal, bullying, and isolation. She became my door to belonging. Always by my side, she lovingly accepted her role as my comforter and protector. Her presence was pure and straightforward—a refreshing change from the people who had mocked and belittled me. Tully didn't deceive or gaslight. She had no hidden agenda. She asked no questions—she didn't need to because she already knew the answers. Through her superpower of scent detection, she could smell my joy, sadness, anger, and fear. We shared the same emotions, mine reflected in hers.

Parker Palmer, renowned Quaker writer, teacher, and activist, sums up the essence of authentic connection with this thought: "The human soul doesn't want to be advised, fixed, or saved. It simply wants to be witnessed—to be seen, heard, and companioned exactly as it is." While not specifically written about animals, Palmer perfectly describes our remarkable bond with dogs: it is a simple, compassionate presence. And that is precisely what Tully gave me. She was content to quietly sit with me and hold my pain in confidence until I was ready to move on.

My restoration began when I realized that my deepest scars stemmed from betrayal. My work with service dogs and veterans with PTSD had pointed me toward that awareness when I witnessed their anger melt away in the presence of a dog. I noticed a similar transformation in myself. While the source of my betrayal was different from a veteran's, we held similar emotional wounds. Both veterans and whistleblowers confront powerful organizations. That process inflicts deep psychological wounds when our experiences clash with our moral compass. We both face similar struggles with betrayal and isolation, and we both have a deep distrust of institutions and people in general, not just those causing the betrayal.

Veterans and whistleblowers often suffer from insomnia and hypervigilance. Following physical threats to my safety, extreme alertness became my reality. It was mentally and physically exhausting to constantly be on high alert. Tully's calming presence helped me through this period. Her heightened senses alerted me to anything unusual, like strangers approaching. In essence, she became my early warning system so that I could be less vigilant. For veterans and whistleblowers, whose sense of security has been damaged, dogs can restore a feeling of safety: one more step on the path back to a normal life.

Retaliation and public misunderstanding of our actions further compound the trauma felt by veterans and whistleblowers and make healing incredibly challenging. Dogs offer an alternative form of therapy for all of this trauma. Research confirms that positive relationships, even across species, rewire neural pathways shaped by trauma. The trust cultivated with Tully was my bridge toward reengaging with people and restoring faith in myself. My most precious gift helped me to trust again, gently guiding me through the process of rebuilding resilience. So much more than a pet, Tully was, and continues to be, my lifeline.

In September 2025, I was honored to be invited to the annual Whistleblowers of America conference. I had the opportunity to speak about my experience, specifically the resilience I had rebuilt through the healing presence of my dog. With Tully by my side, my first order of business was to thank the audience of whistleblowers for inviting me into their family. I had found a group of kindred souls, and for the first time in a long while, I belonged. My new whistleblowing family is scattered across continents, but we have all sailed the same ocean aboard different ships. We share an unbreakable, battle-tested bond of truth, courage, and resilience. I felt right at home.

Stones

You threw stones at me,
Only small ones, at first.
I asked you why?

You tried to bury me
With spirit-crushing boulders.
I told you to stop!

You put a blindfold on me
So that I could not witness your evil.
I could feel it.

You put a gag over my mouth
So I could not tell of your lies.
You thought I would speak.

I did speak.
Those stones & boulders,
That blindfold, that gag
Could not stop me.

After a decade
That crushing burden has lifted.
Now you will feel the weight
Of your lies revealed in the light.

(December 14, 2024, after the Department of Justice
intervened on the case)

CHAPTER 11

Simplicity

*"But I know, somehow, that only when it is
dark enough can you see the stars."*
— **Martin Luther King Jr.**

Our family survived. I survived. Our son had been ripped from our lives, but, inch by inch, we clawed our way back to the land of the living, still on our knees, but breathing after the greatest loss of all. Strength, power, and perspective come from surviving.

I was amazed that I had survived such a profound loss and still had fight left in me. I didn't feel invincible—I was too wise for that—but I did believe that challenges in my future would pale in comparison to the loss of a child. I let go of the incessant anxiety about the case because anxiety served no useful purpose. I forged a new path, and I had a "golden" reason to move forward. But the choices and concessions I continued to make were still dictated by the whistleblower case.

In the no man's land of litigation, I had neither lost nor won, and still the case dragged on. Going into the eighth year since the filing of the first lawsuit, out of necessity, we had become accustomed to frugality. Uprooting our family from the place our children had grown up and where we had fostered friendships for 30 years was a difficult transition, but the uncertainty of my financial future weighed heavily on me. I knew that if the case didn't resolve for several more years, we would be forced to move again. Better to make this decision while the housing market was still affordable. The 30-mile distance from our lifelong community felt like 300. In hindsight, that move out of suburbia and into rural America proved to be my saving grace in many unexpected ways.

Nothing brings discipline into focus more than the necessity of frugality. Wants and needs are clearly delineated. While working in pharma, I'd become accustomed to the luxury of buying things I liked, for no other reason than I liked them and could afford them. With that lifestyle behind me, I only bought what we needed. Period. There was no discretionary spending. Going out to eat, shopping at the mall, going to the movies—all of that vanished. It sounds harsh, but living in the country made some of those choices easier. There was only one stoplight, no shopping mall, no movie theatre, and nowhere to buy anything other than the basics. In exchange for the lost conveniences, we benefitted from a small, close-knit group of neighbors who looked out for each other, traded fresh eggs for homemade bread, took care of each other's animals, visited over a cup of coffee or a glass of wine, and brought food and consolation to us as we mourned the loss of our son.

This Mayberry lifestyle also brought me great comfort. Surrounded by farms with cattle, several horses, two pot-bellied pigs, one bull, a mule, and multiple dogs and cats was what my Pippi heart longed for. Being among the animals and nature brought me solace just as the blackberry patch had. Helping a neighbor wrangle a runaway mule, finding a lost dog in an ice storm, or celebrating the 80th birthday of a neighbor was more appealing to me than the keeping-up-with-the-Joneses lifestyle of suburbia. This neighbor-helping-neighbor community I stumbled upon became a sea of calm in the marathon of litigation.

While there's plenty of research on the money–happiness connection, I associated money with security. In my mind, money and emotional security were and remain deeply intertwined. As the money in my life became ever scarcer, I felt increasingly less secure, both financially and emotionally, probably echoing how my parents had felt, born into poverty during the Great Depression. They faced profound economic insecurity, leading to lifelong habits of thrift, resilience, and a deep fear of returning to poverty. They developed strong self-reliance, determination, and a unique capability to survive and thrive despite early hardship. They were survivors. My parents passed the Depression generation values of a strong work ethic, aversion to waste, and appreciation for security to their baby boomer children, my siblings and me, and for that I will always be grateful.

I can attribute my own resilience and determination to the example of my father, who had experienced significant hardship in his early life. Surrendered to an orphanage, along with his brother, because his parents could not afford to care for them during the Depression, his determination to rise above his lot in life set him up for success in his later years. Throughout the whistleblowing process and its aftermath, I often thought about my parents, specifically my dad, drawing on his example to help me overcome the worry and sleepless nights associated with my family's financial insecurity.

As the years of unemployment and underemployment rolled by, my frugality mindset became one of deprivation. My sustained lack of income affected not only the place where we lived, but the cars we drove, how far we could drive, the food we ate, and my healthcare. Everything I did (or did not do) was directly attributable to my lack of income, which was entirely due to blacklisting. At the grocery store, everyday staples became too expensive for us to afford, so things like meat and yogurt became once-a-week splurges. I learned to make my own soap, shampoo, detergent, and household cleaners. One thing I never skimped on, though, was my dogs' nutrition. They often ate better than we humans did, a testament to the depth of my love for them.

Following my departure from corporate America, healthcare costs skyrocketed, leaving me with few choices. For several years, I was enrolled in public healthcare, but even that was unsustainable. Between the monthly premiums and outrageous copays, I couldn't afford to use the insurance I was paying for. For almost a decade, I had no health insurance at all. That, more than anything else, almost broke me psychologically. The possibility that I was only one life-altering accident or illness away from ruin, or possibly death, made me feel more vulnerable and destitute than all of the other deprivations combined.

I also learned to diminish my own physical and emotional needs to survive. Clothing, food, and warmth fell into the want versus need category. In a span of 10 years, I bought one brand new (not thrifted) piece of clothing: a dress for my son's wedding. Even that was purchased at a Macy's 75% off sale. But it did look fabulous on me! Meals were minimal, but enough to survive on—a sandwich or a bowl of soup. We kept the house uncomfortably cool in the winter, just enough to keep the pipes from freezing, and balmy in the summer, barely enough to take the edge off the sweltering summer humidity.

Eventually, even love and joy fell into the want, not need, category. Relationships and happiness faded to be replaced by cordiality. I was in survival mode in every sense of the word. I had been stripped bare. And for what? To force a pharmaceutical company into abandoning its profit model for accountability? What a ridiculous idea. I tried not to dwell on it, but it was looking less and less likely that anything or anyone would be held accountable for their corruption.

If this sounds like austerity, it was. And as much as I tried to put on a brave face, it was defeating and demoralizing. But in that desert of deprivation, something beautiful arose: simplicity—profound, quiet simplicity. It taught me to reach within myself for what I needed most: creativity, joy, and hope topped my list.

Following my mother's death, I became the heir to her art supplies: acrylic paints, watercolors, charcoals, pastels and oils, canvases, and paper. With zero expectations and no training, I started to paint. And of course, I started with dogs. Looking back, the initial results were, shall we say, unfortunate. My five-year-old granddaughter declared that my first dog painting looked like a beaver! With that honest assessment, the challenge was on. I eventually developed some skill, and painting became an emotional and physical outlet as well as a connection to others. I found joy through creativity, something that probably would not have happened absent the backdrop of simplicity.

Sharing that simple life with my granddaughter had a way of smudging out negativity and replacing it with optimism. The wonder of experiencing things through a child's eyes lifted me up immensely. Feisty, inquisitive, and playful, Claire was the embodiment of laughter and all things good and pure in the world.

My husband and I cherished our roles as Grandan and Nona. I shared with her my passion for creativity, art, baking, and animals. She learned the importance of respect and love for all creatures. She witnessed new farm life emerge each spring, with calves and ducklings, and old life pass away as the neighbors mourned their animals lost to age and infirmity. She quickly grasped how to call horses, feed a mule, and love a dog. I taught her how to recognize boundaries and emotions in animals, and quite possibly herself, too. How I wish I had learned those things as a very young child.

Her Grandan, always full of fantastical stories, fed her imagination. As a toddler, she would look to me for confirmation of his wild tales. I would often tell her, "Grandan is full of bologna!" to which she would laugh uncontrollably. The literal image of an adult being stuffed from head to toe with bologna is a very funny thing to a child. Inevitably, that became one of our favorite games, Truth or Bologna. It worked like this: one person would tell a story, fact or fiction, and it was up to the listeners to decide if it was truth or bologna. It fed her imagination, developed her language and listening skills, and above all, it was fun! No special equipment, no timeframe, and really, no rules. It was simplicity, creativity, and connection. As she got older, the wild tales would contain elements of truth *and* bologna, and she had to discern one from the other. In hindsight, that silly little game was a powerful skill passed down to our granddaughter: the ability to tell truth from lies.

Kids and dogs have a unique ability to draw you into the present. They demand attention in the here and now, not the what-ifs and worries of the past or future. They are among the most vulnerable and needy creatures, and in that I recognized myself. I could easily connect to both and felt fully accepted in their worlds.

Gradually, I replaced my scarcity mindset with gratitude for what was in my life, not what was out of my reach. One of the greatest joys in this season of my life was being Nona to my precious grandchild. The other joy centered on the gift of Tully. I may have lacked financial stability, but they both helped me rebalance through gratitude. Knowing that I was needed, wanted, and unconditionally loved made these two relationships unlike any others in my life.

After 10-plus years of battling corporate corruption, greed, and its aftermath, I was weary of the fight. In the course of that decade, I had also discovered, and humbly accepted, an unexpected path of healing: the unconditional love and presence of a dog. Tully offered redemption from the whistleblowing insecurity and guided me to a reinvented life far more fulfilling than I could have imagined.

We had become an extraordinary team. As I continued with her service dog training, she was training me to sit quietly in the silence of my damaged soul. Her unconditional love was an invitation to extend the same compassion, patience, and acceptance to myself. Her trusting nature encouraged me to trust again—the first step back to wholeness.

Tully responded with empathy to my despair in the professional and personal mountains I faced during this unsettled time. Everything seemed easier with her by my side—sleep, gratitude, and finding purpose beyond the legal process. More than any other factor during this damaging decade, Tully was my refuge and rescue as I navigated some of life's deepest wounds. Through the love of a dog, I was rebuilding resilience and rising from the shadows. Things were looking up, and my future was about to change.

Shiny v. Matte

Everyone wants shiny—
Shiny car, shiny house, shiny life.
I am the opposite of shiny—
Matte but not flat.

I fade into background...
No longer shy, but quiet
In an observant way.
Watching, learning, hearing.

I am witness to a shiny world
But I don't reflect it
Because I don't want to
Or need to.

Steady and strong in observation
My reflection is through empathy
Your pain becomes my pain.
We become one.

My matte exterior
Beckons you closer.
I will not vainly reflect you,
I will embrace you.

(March 2025, as the third whistleblower lawsuit is coming to an end, and I can now connect with others who have suffered retaliation)

CHAPTER 12

Breakthrough Pain

"You can't always get what you want, but if you try sometimes, you'll find you get what you need."
—The Rolling Stones

In early 2024, like the intermittent grinding of ball bearings on an axle gone bad, texts from my lawyer began to pop up about the whistleblower case. Another six-month extension, and then silence. Noise, and then no noise. I could sense that something was happening, but couldn't quite locate the source, or whether it was a good noise or a bad one.

I steeled myself for the bad because that's how my brain was wired. Creating alternative plans for the "what if" of disappointing news had become my survival mechanism. My childhood experience of growing up in an unpredictable and volatile home trained my brain to be hyperaware of emotional signs to protect myself. Texting took away all those cues. A text doesn't reveal tone of voice, direction of eye gaze, or body posture. I had become so fluent in reading human body language that I barely noticed my awareness as a self-defense strategy.

Perhaps this self-preservation skill is why reading canine body language and teaching others about it came so naturally to me. It was truly second nature. Thinking like a dog was often easier than thinking like a human. Dogs are clear, consistent, and trustworthy in their communication and unconditional love. Even at four years old, I had already figured out that adults were confusing, inconsistent, and mostly unavailable.

To escape the situation as a child, I had viewed invisibility as a game, with my dog the only one who could see me. As an adult, feeling "invisible" took the form of dismissal, underestimation, and deep feelings of unworthiness, probably rooted in that very early emotional neglect. The only one to break through the adult cloak of invisibility was, once again, my dog. I allowed my vulnerable self to be seen most fully by Tully, whose soulful brown eyes could easily penetrate my damaged soul and comfort me during this period of turmoil. A human friend or two also overcame those invisible walls, and I will always cherish their insight. They saw something valuable in me that I couldn't find in myself through the fog and aftermath of litigation.

As a very young girl, my sensitivity and compassion allowed me to detect all types of emotional distress in others, both human and canine. And with that recognition, I felt the need to be a protector to those in distress. Defaulting to my compassionate nature and duty of responsibility, even at a very young age, I became the protector of my younger sister and any vulnerable creature that I encountered. Five decades later, that responsibility of protection extended to those damaged by pharmaceutical companies, including the families who were heartbroken by their personal loss due to pain medication addiction.

Since 2014, I had been waiting for a sign that a resolution would finally be found, offering the protection I sought for myself and for those harmed by the pharmaceutical industry. With each random text from my lawyers, I held my breath—was this the one that would validate the decade-long struggle?

January 26, 2024

DOJ is going to give them (Depomed) a few more months in the hopes they will settle.

June 6, 2024

The government got another seal extension a couple of weeks back to continue negotiating.

June 10, 2024

All indications are settlement (not dismissal).

Now, we were beginning to make progress. Or were we? With each requested extension, a settlement seemed farther and farther away, like a racing greyhound chasing a mechanical rabbit, tantalizingly out of reach.

During this period, my father's health was rapidly declining. It was so incredibly sad to witness his wonderfully analytical mind reduced to rubble by the scourge of Alzheimer's. Inch by inch, he lost his ability to think clearly, speak in full sentences, or take care of his own basic needs. His last year on this earth was fraught with the sadness of the emotional and physical battle that stole him from us one small piece at a time. Since the case was still under seal, I couldn't share the details with him. I doubt he would've understood the gravity of the story even if I had told him. But this he did understand: the powerful feeling of being loved and cherished. With every daily visit, I held his hand, told him how proud I was to be his daughter, and how much he meant to me. On June 24, two days after his 93rd birthday, he took his last breath, and I lost my hero. My lifelong model of courage and resilience was gone.

Nine days later, still mourning the loss of my father, I received the following text:

July 3, 2024

The government is filing its motion to intervene. They will be filing their own complaint which will be much more limited in scope than the one that we filed. Your name will be publicly available soon and likely in a press release in the coming weeks.

This good news came as a huge surprise. I could hardly believe what I was reading! The good (government intervention) far outweighed the bad (limited in scope). I was elated and felt a huge weight lift off me. After almost a decade, the DOJ was *finally* going to make a positive move on justice. With that news came a deluge of unanswered questions. The lawyer, on vacation and eating ice cream (his words, not mine), assured me he'd call me the next day with all the details.

The next day came and went—no call and no communication. None the next day. None the next, and the next, and so on. It was a full six days before the lawyer called me. I had waited almost 10 years for this news and was then dropped like a hot potato. What a Bozohead! Apparently, I was a lower priority than ice cream!

Hearing that my name would be in the news concerned me, especially after the debacle of my name being released in the first *qui tam* lawsuit and the subsequent threats to my safety. Watching my back was now routine for me, and not only because of the whistleblower lawsuit. I had grown up looking for emotional and behavioral cues that a verbal or physical assault was on the horizon.

Every day, I scanned legal websites for the release of my name and lawsuit information. The case had been partially unsealed, but it would take almost another full year to be released to the general public. During that timeframe, other news reports began to surface of pain management physicians with ties to Depomed who had violated the False Claims Act. These physicians were accused of breaching the Anti-Kickback Statute by prescribing drugs in exchange for receiving paid speaking and consulting work from drug manufacturers (a very common illegal practice in the pharmaceutical industry). It was exactly the scenario both the co-relator and I had testified to in our relator meetings years ago. I felt hopeful that this news cycle of publicly naming and charging the perpetrators would continue in my whistleblower case.

And then, once again, silence. I'd reach out occasionally to see if there was any update, and I'd get a text about another seal extension. The information vacuum was a powerful anxiety producer. I was craving some kind of feedback—anything—but there was absolutely nothing until mid-fall 2024.

October 3, 2024

Defense counsel has suggested mediation to close the gap.

What gap? This could only mean that the two sides were finally talking about financial punishment. The amount of money the DOJ was asking for in civil fines and what Depomed was willing to pay must have been worlds apart. Throughout the course of this entire whistleblowing process, lawyers had occasionally thrown out a settlement figure of $60–70 million. Previous cases with similar products (gabapentin and fentanyl) resulted in civil fines of $50–200 million and occasionally criminal fines on top of that. As the case dragged on, the guesstimated figure dwindled to around $20 million.

In *qui tam* False Claims Act cases, relators are entitled to a percentage of the civil fine for bringing reliable evidence to the government. In addition, the relators have to be the first to file, meaning they were the first to report the false claims, and the information had to have been previously unknown to the government. With all those stipulations satisfied, it was up to the government to decide the percentage of the civil fine to be shared with the informants.

While the case was always about holding Depomed accountable for their lies and fraud, the thought that I might be able to afford some of the necessities of life gave me hope. Necessities, not luxuries: shoes with no holes, a roof that didn't leak, and a car I could afford to gas up. Feeling confident that I had contributed substantial, damning physical evidence and testimony against Depomed, I found myself back on the hopeful roller coaster.

December 1, 2024

We're getting closer to settlement...do you think you could put together a paragraph or so about any retaliation you faced...bullet points will work. I'll need it first thing in the morning. There's mediation going on, and we need to get your claim in the mix.

I welcomed any positive news, and this definitely fell into that category. Wasn't there a 149-page complaint that already laid all this out? A paragraph of bullet points to describe the effects of 10 years of retaliation? Once again, I felt utterly devalued, but if this was my last chance to take a stand, I was going to make it count.

Well into the early morning hours, I read and reread the 2018 amended complaint and pulled out the highlights of Depomed's retaliation against me. Rereading the details was deeply traumatic because it psychologically threw me back into the proverbial fire. The feelings of corporate betrayal came flooding back with such intensity that it shocked me. But before 8 a.m. the next morning, Mr. Bozohead had four pages of bullet points and a color-coded timeline of the retaliation, culminating in my constructive discharge in June 2013. I had not only fulfilled the request but, in usual fashion, had given him more than he had asked for. Now it was up to him to fight like hell for the case and for me.

The next day involved an equally onerous task. The lawyer needed a dollar figure for all the retaliation I had endured. This task was far more difficult because I had no idea how to calculate a decade's worth of lost back pay plus interest, healthcare, benefits, and, of course, emotional suffering. This was also needed by the next morning. My eyes popped at the number as I calculated and re-calculated the figures. By my numbers, the retaliation against me, barring emotional suffering, exceeded $2 million! That was a stunning and depressing amount of money. There it was, in black and white—this was what telling the truth had cost me. I submitted all the paperwork and calculations by the next morning. The ongoing, confidential negotiations and daily requests for more information needed ASAP continued throughout the first week of December 2024. And then I got the news on which I had staked my entire professional career and moral integrity.

December 6, 2024, 5:08 p.m.

The federal government settled the case today for $3.6 million.

I sat in stunned silence, staring at the text. The dreary cold of early December and the pittance of a settlement hit me all at once. I was dumbfounded. There weren't enough tissues in my house to hold the buckets of tears I cried that night. Thinking of the 10-plus years of trial and tribulation, and all of the families who had also suffered at the hands of the pharmaceutical industry's fraudulent opioid marketing, made me sick to my stomach.

For a case that was originally valued at 10 to 20 times the final settlement amount, this punishment was less than a slap on the wrist. It felt more like a secret handshake between two players on the same team. While it was a win for the government, Depomed also won through technicalities and procedural delays. In my opinion, they got away with murder, and every American paid the price.

Shattered

The shattered bits
Of rose-colored glass
Surround me
Moving forward cuts deeply

There is no shortcut.
If I stay,
I will die
The blood is rising.

Move now
Find a path
Before it's too late
The world is waiting

(June 26, 2024, two days after my father's death and one week before the DOJ intervened in the case)

CHAPTER 13

Bad Good Friday

"I see the bad moon a-rising
I see trouble on the way
I see earthquakes and lightning
I see bad times today"
—"Bad Moon Rising,"
Creedence Clearwater Revival

With time, most terrible news has a way of softening. But the confidential secret handshake deal between the Department of Justice and Depomed was not sitting well with me. There was no softening, only more questions. The government's financial analysis of Depomed determined that $3.6 million was all Depomed could afford to pay. Cue the violins. Predictably, there were no other details. That was it. That was all Depomed could afford. In essence, sit down, shut up, and don't ask any more questions.

Following this negotiation, the government was in the position of determining the percentage of the fine to be doled out to the relators. The range established by law on *qui tam* False Claims Act lawsuits was 15–25% of the government's settlement. My lawyers assured me that my co-relator and I would be "taken care of."

On December 18, word came down from on high that the amount allotted to us was 18.5%. This time, the news was delivered by a telephone call rather than a text. The lawyers immediately began their expected self-aggrandizing routine: "We worked so hard for you to get such a high percentage. The government wanted to offer 18%, but we got them to 18.5."

Are you f***ing kidding me? Such a high percentage? That is what I might have expected if I had shown up at Panera 10 years ago, dropped off my envelope of information with the lawyer, and said, "Call me when it's over." I was heavily involved in the writing of all three complaints, prepared and participated fully in three separate relator meetings, and traveled across the country for one of those meetings. I was not an uninvolved participant, spending hundreds upon hundreds of hours on the case over the past ten years. My entire life had been upended for a decade through the whistleblowing process. And, to be clear, that 18.5% portion of the settlement was not my portion alone. It was to be divided four ways: the lawyers got first cut, then the co-relator, then me, and last but certainly not least, Uncle Sam. What the government giveth, the government taketh.

But all was not lost, not yet anyway. Although the Depomed–DOJ deal was done, there was still another portion of the lawsuit to be addressed—the retaliation claim. This negotiation was solely between Depomed and my lawyers. At this point, the government had received what it had asked for and stepped away from the negotiating table. Now it was up to my lawyers to go head-to-head with the Depomed legal team and hammer out the details of compensation for the retaliation that the relators had suffered. Similar to the pre-Christmas rush of ASAP document gathering and submission, the process began again in earnest.

Retaliation against a whistleblower is illegal, and the companies that are caught doing it pay steep compensation to those they have harmed. Federal laws like the False Claims Act (FCA) and the Sarbanes-Oxley Act (SOX) are designed to protect corporate whistleblowers, along with a host of state laws designed to do the same thing—protect whistleblowers from retaliation. It is because of this legal quagmire that choosing a lawyer well-versed in these whistleblower protections is essential. You wouldn't choose a family practice doctor to perform neurosurgery. The same principle applies to whistleblower law. The stipulations, deadlines, and procedural requirements are strict and non-negotiable.

During a February 2025 conference call, the lawyers requested a whole host of new (and old) documentation. Having gone through this process less than a month earlier, I thought I had sent them everything, but they wanted more. To justify my claim for back compensation plus interest, the largest portion of the retaliation claim, the lawyers wanted 12 years of back tax returns. This was a bear of a task and involved calling accountants, some of whom had passed away, and filling out paperwork for the IRS. Incredulous that I could survive on so little income, another lawyer was added to the case to double-check my figures. I understood the need for accuracy, but this was a low blow, underscoring the fact that my family had greatly suffered financially. It was definitely a case of kicking a woman while she was down.

During all the back and forth of this intense period, the lawyers determined that my figures were, in fact, inaccurate. The previous $2 million I had estimated in retaliation had been recalculated to a whopping $4 million. The cost of telling the truth—$4 million! I didn't know whether to be thankful for the adjusted figure or exponentially devastated. Every single dollar of that $4 million was money I had taken away from my family and my future. In order to fight the bigger fight and take a stand for truth, I had essentially bankrupted those I loved the most. I was heartbroken.

As this phase was winding down, I received a text from Mr. Bozohead requesting details of the split of settlement money between me and the co-relator. I, of course, had all of the documents dating back to 2011 and could easily get him the information he needed. I remember thinking at the time how odd that request was. Did his office not have a copy of the signed contract? Wouldn't it have been easier to ask the paralegal to get that information for him? No matter, I thought to myself, and passed the information along.

An uneasy feeling was starting to creep in as I began to replay the events and settlement over the last couple of months. Why were the lawyers requesting the same documents just weeks apart? Why were they so quick to defend themselves regarding the 18.5% settlement as such a great feat when, in reality, it was not? Why were they not offering any significant explanation about the insignificant $3.6 million settlement? It wasn't adding up. I was beginning to feel that things were not going as well as the lawyers were leading me to believe.

If there was one thing in my life that I was sure of, it was my intuition. Even when I didn't want to acknowledge the uneasy feeling, it was still there. Like the days of my childhood, waiting for criticism to pour over me, I could feel it coming. Like the retaliation in corporate America, I could feel it coming. Like the smell of rain before a storm hits, you know it's coming. I could sense the storm approaching.

With all the retaliation documents submitted, the waiting game began again. Still scanning the legal websites for any mention of the case, I found some unexpected news. The updated docket showed that the case was stayed for another 60 days. No call from the lawyers, no communication whatsoever, and there it was. Déjà-vu all over again. How long would this round of the torturous waiting game last, and why had I not been informed? I could now hear a distant rumble of thunder.

Over the next several weeks, multiple calls and texts bounced back and forth, but they seemed positive and hopeful about a successful outcome regarding the retaliation claim—a distinctly different tone from before. Maybe I had misjudged the lawyers. Maybe I was too skeptical to see the life-changing outcome that was only weeks away. I tried to squash all the unsettled feelings, but they just kept popping back up like a Whack-A-Mole game. I attributed it to stress, fatigue, anxiety, and anything other than my highly accurate intuition. Lightning was now beginning to appear on the horizon.

After several weeks of no communication, I received an unusual early morning text.

Friday, April 18, 7:27 a.m.

Do you have time to talk to us today? Is 3:30 ok?

I had always made myself available to the lawyers on their schedule, but on this particular day, I wanted to refuse. It was Good Friday, the most solemn day on the Christian calendar. Easter is my favorite liturgical holiday. Everything about it speaks to me: redemption, second chances, and new beginnings. Even the solemnity of Good Friday echoed in my own life—the sorrow before the joy, the false accusations, the death of oneself in search of a higher ideal. I wanted to attend Good Friday service, but instead acquiesced and agreed to the conference call. I thought Jesus would understand, especially since it involved "the good news" that I was expecting.

Within seconds of hearing the lawyer's voice, I knew this was not going to be a celebration or redemption or even a second chance.

"They said they have no intention of settling this case," Ben began.

Lightheartedly, I jumped in, "Of course they don't. Who wants to admit wrongdoing and shell out several million dollars?" I anticipated the conversation would turn toward a reduced settlement.

Ben continued, "No, they're not going to pay anything at all. There will be no retaliation money."

My brain struggled to register the unexpected message. Deep breath. "How can that be? What are you saying? For the last several weeks, all you could talk about was the settlement money." I could hear the desperation in my own voice.

Ben: "It was a technicality. They said we missed the deadline to file."

I felt like I was playing a game of 20 questions: "Which deadline?"

Ben: "The deadline to file a retaliation claim. It needed to be filed within three years."

Me: "It was filed within three years. The first case was filed in 2014, one year after the retaliation."

Ben: "That case was dismissed."

I desperately searched for any logical or legal reason that his information couldn't possibly be true. No matter what I threw out, he countered.

Finally, he said the words I never thought I would hear: "It's over. We lost."

"We lost" hit me like a wrecking ball. I was shocked into silence. I had no response, nothing. I was numb. I felt like my brain had short-circuited because there were no words. Eventually, I could feel the anger and frustration rising and the tears falling. I remained silent in disbelief. Ben made an attempt to diffuse the tension with humor by acknowledging that it was

Good Friday and he was going to eat a pound of pork. It wasn't funny. My voice cracked as I said goodbye.

I could feel the weight of this solemn day, and the words "we lost" played over and over in my head. I just couldn't process all the shock, sadness, and disappointment at once. I sat alone in my office staring at the boxes of Depomed paperwork and evidence cluttering the floor. What was this all for? I wanted to burn it all down, erase the past and all the baggage that came with it. For 11 years, I had been mocked, condemned, threatened with death, and then abandoned. Stripped to the core. Battle-worn and bloody. On that Good Friday, I felt the weight of the cross as I had never felt before.

Bad Good Friday

I died today
A little bit more
How could there be anything left
To wither and fall away?

It is not inconsequential
That today is Good Friday,
The most solemn of holy days
Full of sorrow and pain and death.

I think of Jesus
Not because I am like Him
But I feel the weight of His suffering too
In addition to my own.

I fought for truth
I put everything into the battle
And in the end
Fraud and lies won.

Was this the plan:
To condemn me, to abandon me?
It has been a brutal decade
Almost everything has been lost
Almost.

(Good Friday, April 18, 2025, 4:00 p.m.)

CHAPTER 14

Settlement

"These days the buck stops nowhere
No one takes the blame
But evil is still evil
In anybody's name."
—"If Dirt Were Dollars," Don Henley

A technicality. My future was lost on a technicality. Seeing this in print still hurts me today. Not lost on the merits of the claim. There was no debating whether I had suffered retaliation. Like a back-handed compliment, my years of retaliation were, by default, acknowledged but quickly dismissed, found to be unworthy of review.

In predictable psychological angst, I blamed myself. How could I have not seen this coming? What could I have done differently? I felt that I had let so many people down, not the least of which was my family. The suffering that I had caused them by dragging them through a decade-long litigation process was soul-crushing. Spinning further down the lonely spiral of despair, I thought about the families who had lost loved ones in the throes of opioid addiction and the communities that battled the effects of Big Pharma corruption due to the dumping of illegally marketed pain medication into their lives.

Also, in a predictable fashion, Tully stayed close as I worked through the destructive process of self-blame. She would frequently use her most powerful consolation tactic: gently placing her head in my lap and looking directly into my eyes until I acknowledged her presence. She could feel my utter defeat and stayed with me night and day. Tully was not going to let me drown alone.

As with each previous defeat, trauma, and tragedy, the time came to pick myself up off the floor. And again, self-reflection led me back to betrayal and truth. I had done everything I could to gather evidence and initiate a legal case. I had poured every ounce of myself into a successful outcome. The problem was not me at all. I had been betrayed by my lawyers, who had failed me. I had been betrayed by the legal system in general, corporate America, my colleagues, and the healthcare system. They had all worked together for mediocrity and maintaining the status quo, not for truth and justice. That was a bitterly honest pill to swallow.

The flashing neon sign above my head read "unworthy." For if I had been worthy, I wouldn't have been betrayed. I was back in the blackberry patch, undeserving of even the most basic human needs of love and connection. Those primal emotions were raw, powerful, and unjustly magnified as I floundered, vulnerable and hurt.

My logical brain tried to find solace in the fact that I had done the right thing, but the message was drowned out by my emotional brain rehashing the previous 11 years. Ever so slowly, the "what went wrong?" analysis was being replaced by the "what's next?" phase, and that entailed signing the requisite legal settlement paperwork.

Still numb from the pain of defeat, the lawyers left me alone to lick my wounds. After two weeks, they initiated contact about the legal documents that needed to be signed, warning me that the government could renege on their end of the deal (18.5%) if I refused to sign. Rather than a conciliatory tone, the communication felt confrontational and threatening. Assuring me that the contract was standard legal jargon, they just wanted me to sign so they could move on. Wary of any assurance from this legal team, I took great care to read the entire document. I had questions, and I wanted answers.

Unlike our previous calls, where I simply received and accepted their information, I had some pointed questions and would not accept vagueness. I was on the offense this time, and I wasn't going to back down until I got to the bottom of this fiasco. As far as I was concerned, we were no longer on the same team.

They had destroyed my foundational belief that they would protect me, fight for me, and keep me safe in the legal process. It wasn't the first time in my life that my assumption about someone having my best interests at heart had shattered me to my core. All these thoughts swirled around me as we talked for the first time since the verdict had been handed down.

I got right to the point: "What did Depomed counsel mean when they said we didn't file in time?"

Ben jumped right in. He was the last lawyer to join the legal team in 2018 when the amended complaint was filed, and the co-relator joined the case; obviously, he had been anticipating the question. "By the time I joined the team, the complaint had already been filed."

Not fully understanding the significance of that answer, I pressed further. "It was filed in 2014. Why doesn't that count? Is there any continuation clause from one case to another?"

"No. The retaliation claim wasn't filed in the three-year time frame." Ben repeated his earlier statement, "By the time I joined the team, the complaint had already been filed."

My mind was racing. I could hear myself getting louder and more annoyed that he kept repeating the same thing. I wanted a real answer.

Agitated, I interrupted my own train of thought to address his repeated statement. "Why do you keep saying that? The facts are the facts; they've never changed. I was retaliated against, and the evidence was clear."

Ben finally got to the crux of the matter. "A retaliation claim wasn't included in the first complaint. It wasn't added until 2018, and by then, it was too late. The statute of limitations had run out."

I thought my head was going to explode. "What do you mean it wasn't included? I was forced to resign because they made it impossible for me to do my job. It was a clear-cut case of constructive discharge."

Ben was now silent, and Mr. Bozohead spoke up. "It wasn't included."

"Why not?" I practically shouted into the phone.

"I didn't think it was that important," Bozohead flatly responded.

"Not important?" I was definitely shouting by now. "The fact that they systematically destroyed me and my future career was not important?" I forcefully confronted his dismissive tone. "You are the lawyer. You should've recognized it. You should've filed in time. You have failed me. A decade of working together, and you have 100% failed me."

Ben jumped in to calm the seas, but by then, it was too late. The truth had been spoken. I felt utterly violated. "Look, I know you're angry, and you want to blame someone..."

Before he could go any further with whatever conciliatory nonsense he was going to spout, I cut him off. "Damn right I'm angry, and I have every right to be!" Repeating for a third time, just in case they missed it the first two times, "You have utterly failed me!"

And with failure lingering in the air, our conversation abruptly ended. I don't easily get to a point where I resort to shouting, but I couldn't contain my outrage any longer. In fact, that moment was the first time I had ever stood on the mountaintop of lifelong betrayal, dismissal, and lies and staked my claim. It was going to end here and now. I would no longer be invisible. I was amazed at my own clarity and boldness.

With that emboldened attitude, I approached the final stage of the settlement: signing the paperwork. The government had set a deadline for all the claims to be settled, and we were rapidly approaching that date. The lawyers wanted to wrap things up and be done with me by May 9. As the date approached, the pressure was on to get everything signed, sealed, and delivered. I was hesitant to sign the document, afraid I might regret it later. I had been strong-armed more than once to either sign the settlement agreement or throw away the opportunity to receive any compensation.

I was still not satisfied with the lawyers' explanation and wanted more information, specifically about the failure to file the retaliation claim within the prescribed statute of limitations. In one particularly lengthy email, Ben, perhaps in an effort to absolve his colleagues of their sins, stated that I had been previously informed about this scenario (retaliation claim denial) by the other lawyers involved in the case. In other words, he was questioning my recollection of the events and attempting to create doubt in my mind. The very same lawyers who had previously lauded my recollection of events, conversations, and dates were now trying to gaslight me. You would think after 11 years, they would've thought twice about that tactic.

I wasn't falling for that BS. With just two days to go, I reminded him of the facts.

"At this point, I do not agree with point number three under 'Terms and Conditions,' as there has been no resolution to the retaliation portion of the claim. I do not accept Depomed's argument that the SOL ran out. If it had, then I should have been informed by my legal team in 2017, which I was not. As you are aware, I have a very good memory and keep excellent notes on calls, as well as preserving conversations relevant to this case. I do not believe that the settlement agreement with regard to point number three is either fair or adequate, and I will not be signing the agreement as it stands today."

Friday, May 9, came and went. I did not sign the agreement. I received no text, call, or email from the legal team. I had a feeling they were huddled in a back room somewhere, trying to figure out what to do about me. And I, conversely, was doing the same. I contacted other lawyers who were friends and laid out the scenario. Three separate lawyers said the same thing: missing a statute of limitations is one of the most egregious mistakes that a lawyer can make. (I already knew this from my short foray into the paralegal world.) It usually results in the client losing their case and often leads to a legal malpractice claim against the attorney. They advised me not to sign the settlement agreement because I was in direct conflict with the lawyers who were representing me. You bet I was in conflict! The lawyer friends assured me that the case would go nowhere without my signature and that I needed to consider all alternatives, including a legal malpractice suit.

As the weekend wore on, I was even more conflicted about what to do. On one hand, I was being advised to sign the settlement agreement, or else. On the other hand, I was advised not to sign the agreement, let the chips fall where they may, and sue the legal team for failing to meet the standard of care. As I weighed the pros and cons, I ultimately had to be honest with myself. A $4 million retaliation claim was an astronomical amount of money to walk away from. But several more years of litigation, at my own expense, would bury me emotionally and financially. As much as I wanted to set things right, I didn't have any more fight left in me. It had been a hell of a battle, and I was ready to move on with my life.

On Monday, May 12, 2025, I signed the settlement agreement. Within hours, the Department of Justice published the following:

PRESS RELEASE

Pharmaceutical Manufacturer Assertio Therapeutics Inc. Agrees to Pay $3.6M to Resolve Allegations that It Violated the False Claims Act in Connection with Marketing Its Fentanyl Product

Friday, May 9, 2025

The Justice Department announced today that Assertio Therapeutics Inc., formerly known as Depomed Inc. (Assertio), a pharmaceutical company headquartered in Lake Forest, Illinois, has agreed to pay $3.6 million to resolve claims that Assertio violated the False Claims Act (FCA) by causing the submission of false claims for the transmucosal immediate-release fentanyl (TIRF) drug Lazanda for individuals who did not have breakthrough cancer pain.

Lazanda, a fentanyl nasal spray, is approved by the FDA solely for breakthrough cancer pain in patients who are already receiving and who are tolerant to opioid therapy for their underlying persistent cancer pain. The United States alleges that, between 2013 and 2017, Assertio, which was known as Depomed at the time, caused the submission of false claims to the Medicare and TRICARE programs by focusing its marketing on pain specialists who were prescribing high volumes of TIRF products, including those who were flagged for diversion or who were later indicted. The United States further alleges that Assertio placed high-volume TIRF prescribers on its speakers' bureau and advisory boards and developed its "Signature Support Program" to ensure that Lazanda prescriptions would be approved by insurance companies, including Medicare Part D plans. The United States contends that Assertio's marketing efforts caused prescribers to write Lazanda prescriptions for Medicare and TRICARE beneficiaries who did not have breakthrough cancer pain, resulting in the submission of false claims to Medicare and TRICARE from thirteen high-volume prescribers.

"This company took steps to boost its profits despite the risk of boosting the deadly opioid epidemic," said U.S. Attorney Edward R. Martin Jr. for the District of Columbia. "Our office will continue to seek out violations like this that demonstrate a brazen disregard for the safety of the public."

"At a time when communities across the country are still dealing with the devastating impact of the opioid epidemic, pharmaceutical companies have a responsibility to uphold the highest standards of integrity," said Acting Assistant Director Darren Cox of the FBI's Criminal Investigative

Division. "This settlement reflects the FBI's unwavering commitment to protecting public health and holding those accountable who fuel addiction and defraud federal healthcare programs through deceptive marketing of powerful drugs like fentanyl."

"Violations of the False Claims Act, such as the illegal prescribing practices alleged in this settlement, are especially egregious considering the opioid epidemic," said Deputy Inspector General Christian J. Schrank of the Department of Health and Human Services Office of Inspector General (HHS-OIG). "HHS-OIG will continue to work with our law enforcement partners to ensure health care providers and corporations involved in schemes that threaten patient safety are held accountable."

The civil settlement includes the resolution of claims under the *qui tam*, or whistleblower, provisions of the FCA by Noelle Webb and Nicole Novellino, who previously worked at Assertio as sales representatives. The FCA authorizes private parties to sue on behalf of the United States for false claims and share in any recovery. The *qui tam* case is captioned *United States ex rel. Webb et al. v. Assertio Therapeutics Inc., f/k/a Depomed, Inc.*, No. 1:17-02309 (D.D.C.). The relators' share of these proceeds has not yet been determined.

The Justice Department's Civil Division, Commercial Litigation Branch (Fraud Section), and the U.S. Attorney's

Office for the District of Columbia handled this matter. The Federal Bureau of Investigation, led by its Washington Field Office, the Food and Drug Administration's Office of Criminal Investigations, and the Department of Health and Human Services Office of Inspector General, provided substantial assistance in the investigation and resolution.

Today's settlement illustrates the government's emphasis on combating healthcare fraud. One of the most powerful tools in this effort is the FCA. Tips and complaints from all sources about potential fraud, waste, abuse, and mismanagement can be reported to the Department of Health and Human Services at 800-HHS-TIPS (800-447-8477).

Senior Trial Counsel Sarah Arni, Trial Attorney Matthew Arrow, and Assistant Director Natalie Waites of the Civil Division's Fraud Section and Assistant U.S. Attorney Darrell Valdez for the District of Columbia handled this matter.

The claims resolved by the settlement are allegations only and there has been no determination of liability.

Updated May 12, 2025

The battle was finished, almost 12 years to the day after I had resigned from Depomed. Following 11 years of litigation, it was over. The article highlighted the government's harsh criticism of Depomed, something not usually noted in a DOJ press release: "This company took steps to boost its profits despite the risk of boosting the deadly opioid epidemic ... At a time when communities across the country are still dealing with the devastating impact of the opioid epidemic, pharmaceutical companies have a responsibility to uphold the highest standards of integrity." Exactly my point for the past 11 years. Sadly, though, as the final sentence points out: "The claims resolved by the settlement are allegations only, and there has been no determination of liability." And there never would be. Depomed escaped with only a few scrapes and bruises, while the rest of us were nothing more than stepping stones on the path to profit.

I never spoke directly to the lawyers again. A few texts back and forth, to wrap things up as the case was completed, confirmed that uneasy feeling from six months prior. Mr. Bozohead, living up to his name, couldn't find copies of our original client retainer agreement, nor the signed co-relator agreement, and requested them from me. To lose the foundational documents of our agreement was sloppy and unprofessional. It wasn't much of a stretch to consider that the frenzy over the statute of limitations on the retaliation claim actually was a failure to meet the legal standard of care. By now, however, all of that was troubled water under the bridge.

One Victory

The fight is over
It is time to step back
And move to another realm.
I do not know how to go
Or where to go.

I have lost much
And won little.
The victories were more bitter than sweet.

In the end though,
I was brave.
I did have courage.
And that, my dear, is sweet Victory.

(May 12, 2025, upon signing the settlement agreement)

CHAPTER 15

Intrepid Crusader

"Above all, be the heroine of your life, not the victim." —**Nora Ephron**

The curtain had fallen on that decade of my life. A time that had begun with immense confidence in truth and justice had turned out to be a period fraught with professional and personal upheaval, grief, and disappointment. But it was also a time of rising, becoming, and standing up for others and for myself.

As I tried to move on, disappointment and anger resurfaced with each new article about the misuse of opioids in general and gabapentin in particular, now the seventh most prescribed drug in the U.S. Patients, families, and communities continue to suffer from the fallout of gabapentin overprescribing and pharmaceutical corruption. If the Department of Justice had taken action against this scourge and the big pharma lies a decade ago, we may not be reading those headlines today. By refusing to act in a timely way, the government essentially sanctioned pharmaceutical corruption and placed the overprescription burden squarely on the shoulders of the American public. I still feel the sting of a mission unfinished with each article I read. I mourn the souls lost to addiction. I carry the grief of each family that has suffered, including my own.

With no other legal options available to me, it was time to move on to fighting the more personal battle of overcoming the psychological effects of whistleblowing. Like most whistleblowers whose identities are anchored in integrity, competence, and responsibility, those values of truth-telling had come under heavy attack. During the long haul of litigation, I had become disassociated from these most sacred parts of myself. This was a time of self-reflection and shaking off the emotional baggage that I continued to carry.

One of the first tasks I addressed was my disappointment and acceptance of the settlement. If the case was so inconsequential, as evidenced by the settlement, then by extension, so was I. And by extrapolation, the truth was also inconsequential. Every battle and legal outcome during this past decade carried the message that truth and justice did not matter. I had to uncouple the settlement from the truth, and that hurt. But I also wanted to preserve the only tangible proof that I had actually accomplished anything over the past decade.

My first purchase following settlement? A bar of soap, specifically Dove Men's soap, a reminder of my life before whistleblowing. It felt so extravagant to consider buying something that was not essential for my survival. I stood in the grocery store aisle staring at the grey and green box with white letters, the need versus want conversation playing out so loudly in my head that I was certain anyone nearby could hear it. I didn't really need it, but I wanted it. I put it in my handheld basket and headed toward the checkout—and then turned around and put it back on the shelf. Was I really ready to move on? Was I accepting defeat, or was I boldly taking a step forward? How was it possible that the simple decision to buy or not buy a bar of soap crippled me?

After far too much deliberation, I bought it. That single soap purchase felt like freedom—freedom from Depomed, freedom from litigation, and freedom from corruption. In a sense, I was trying to wash away the anger, grief, and betrayal of trust of the past decade. That bar of soap held so much power! But addressing all of the emotional fallout wouldn't be that easy.

I distanced myself from the legal ties that had bound the lawyers, the co-relator, and me. The lawyers continued with their other cases, and the co-relator continued in pharmaceutical sales. I could never return to that life—the trauma had cut too deeply. To put the painful disappointment of the legal outcome into perspective, I am reminded of a present-day legal hero, Attorney Paul Farrell, Jr., who also recently faced an unexpected professional loss. Following his defeat in a landmark opioid litigation against major drug distributors, his words now ring true in my own life: "The defiance of standing up for what is right outweighs the pain of being told you're wrong." I did stand up for what was right. I was defiant in the face of corruption, and those are noble things.

But I didn't feel noble. Mostly, I felt numb.

Tully was my antidote to numbness. She was a beacon of hope and an agent of healing throughout the litigation. She led me away from the chaos and despair of legal battles to the natural world. She was a potent reminder of my sacred interconnectedness with all living things. Our deep connection guided me toward peace and helped me rebuild myself, step by step. In the face of legal challenges and dismissals, missed deadlines, and lost settlements, Tully remained constant and true, more than the majority of people in my life. Tully became my Leash of Courage.

As I divorced myself from the corporate and legal worlds, Tully continued to be my conduit for healing and transformation, quietly turning my pain into purpose. She reminded me of the value of presence and connection over the institutional deities of speed and efficiency. She embodied the gifts I had been seeking my whole life—unconditional love, trust, loyalty, devotion, forgiveness, belonging, joy, affection, and acknowledgement. Tully represented a bridge between pain and healing. She was and continues to be my living and breathing connection to all things godly and divine.

Those gifts flow both ways. I am acutely aware of her emotional state. If her body language reveals apprehension or anxiety, I respond to her with calming presence; if there's fear, I try to remove the offender to give her a chance to recalibrate and find peace. She is always by my side, and I acknowledge her presence through gentle praise or enthusiastic words, petting, or simply sitting with her. Our emotional needs mirror each other.

As her caretaker, I want her to feel safe, seen, loved, and appreciated—all the critical positive interactions I missed as a very young child.

Whistleblowing was not a career choice. It was a reckoning between me and a corrupt system. I had survived retaliation without surrendering my conscience, but could never return to who I was before. I have changed. The whistleblowing ordeal demanded that I face the lifelong betrayals and disappointments that bled into and framed my mission of justice and truth. To move past mere survival and truly flourish, the inner journey of self-reflection required more work, more courage, rebuilding resilience, and a deep commitment to the process of becoming.

Like most others, I am a work in progress. I continue to struggle with the retaliatory effects of whistleblowing. I still live a shrouded life, with physical and emotional protections in place. I am always vigilant, careful not to expose myself or reveal too much. Human trust is a difficult bridge to cross. Forgiveness is an even higher mountain. It is in this space of recognition that my wounded psyche meets my healing psyche.

I have only recently accepted that my highly sensitive nature is not a liability or a deficit, but a profound gift. It is my superpower. Detecting early warning signs of threat and fleeing to a place of safety is a survival mechanism. It is hard-wired into my DNA. In the corporate world, it allowed me to perceive the early undercurrent of ethical dilemmas and register corruption long before it became publicly known. I instinctively perceived inconsistencies, false messages, and subtleties that colleagues missed or adapted to. I recognized deceptive and manipulative patterns that others refused to acknowledge. I couldn't unsee what I had seen or unhear what I had heard. I couldn't look away from the corruption, and I couldn't collude with it either.

Not only could I identify moral inconsistencies quickly, but I could also predict the consequences of the corruption, feeling a responsibility to stop it and protect those who could be harmed by it. The consequence of Depomed's alleged illegal marketing was the dumping of pain medication into communities, adding fuel to the opioid epidemic and ensuing addiction. I felt a responsibility to stop it. This universal pattern repeats itself in every whistleblower's story: a deep-seated conviction to protect others and themselves from harm. In taking this road less traveled, we ultimately hope to connect to a greater selfless mission and build a more honest community. And this is the paradox of the whistleblower's fate: the world pressures individuals to abandon their inner truth in exchange for belonging. Whistleblowers want to belong too, but we cannot accept this bargain. We refuse it, choose to speak up, vow to protect, and then pay a heavy price in isolation, outside retaliation, and internal self-doubt.

For most of my adult life, friends and family have often told me that I missed my calling, a not-so-subtle swipe at my life choices. I often wondered if they were right; self-doubt flourished in this internal debate. My academic record, combined with a strong desire to protect and heal others, led them to assume that I should've gone into medicine or the veterinary field. While I did consider those professions, I sensed their inherent emotional toll would bury me. I instinctively knew my sensitive soul could only absorb so much pain and suffering; it would shut down and flee. There was a very distinct possibility that if I followed those paths, I would lose the very heart of myself and become invisible, incapable of healing or protecting anyone, including myself. I chose a different path: related, but different. I thought the pharmaceutical industry was a good compromise between my scientific mind and desire to help others; I couldn't have been more wrong. As it turned out, I couldn't compromise on my inherent nature. In that sense, I couldn't have been more right.

In retrospect, I have always protected those who couldn't speak for themselves: those who held no power. As a child, I protected the four-year-old by making her invisible. Throughout my life, I have protected and nurtured the people and dogs who had been discounted and discarded. As an adult, I tried to protect the families who were being ravaged by corporate corruption and its consequences. In essence, I have always been a protector, an advocate, a truth-teller, and so, not surprisingly, I became a whistleblower. It wasn't so much a choice as it was a manifestation of my lifelong personality traits coming together in one perfect storm—empathy, conscientiousness, intelligence, persistence, and intuition, overlaid with a sense of responsibility to protect others. In the full framework of my life, it all makes sense now. I now accept the title recently bestowed on me by a dear friend: "intrepid crusader for truth and justice." I am exactly where I am meant to be and what I am meant to be. I am living out my true calling.

And so, my friends, as you embark on your own journey, I'll share a few pearls of wisdom I learned on mine.

Do not doubt your instincts or your worth. You were born with a heart that knows beauty, truth, and justice. Wherever the road leads you, create a purposeful life guided by your true calling. You'll know it's right when you feel it's right. Don't strive to be normal. Aim for extraordinary and find the hero within yourself. And if you take nothing else from this book, always cherish and guard the profound healing connection with the most magnificent creature sitting right beside you: your dog.

Last Ounce

To continue the battle
Would've consumed me
Last ounce of self
Last glint of spark.

Those tattered remnants
Will rekindle resilience.
There is more to me
Than this shadow version.

I will remain here at the bottom
Temporarily
Searching
For oxygen.

Another life
Will emerge
Slowly
Purposefully
Waiting for me to acknowledge.

(May 27, 2025, end of litigation)

Epilogue

*"When you do things from your soul,
you feel a river moving in you. A joy."*
—Rumi

This is not the end of my story. Unlike others who may have found themselves forever lost in the belly of corporate corruption, that is not my life's definition. Now that the litigation door has firmly closed, other doors have opened. The trials and tribulations of whistleblowing have become an unlikely springboard—a new beginning.

Seventy-one days from beginning to end, from introduction to epilogue. I had begun this book countless times over the past decade, but always got stuck and abandoned the story along the way. Roadblocks in my path stopped me. I didn't know the ending; I couldn't reveal details for legal reasons. Now I see the biggest roadblock was me. My initial outline was too limited—it only involved the pharmaceutical industry's corruption and litigation. But the true beginning of my story goes back much further, all the way back to the blackberry patch. It was there that I found a small girl sitting alone in the brambles with her dog. She always had the spirit of a protector, a fighter, and a crusader, but it took a lifetime to fully develop, recognize, and accept her.

The whistleblower side of this journey has been tumultuous. The personal side has been unsettling, revealing, and totally unforeseen. Paul Coelho, Brazilian lyricist and novelist, frames it beautifully: "We will only understand the miracle of life fully when we allow the unexpected to happen." During the past 71 days, I have allowed the unexpected into my life through writing and self-reflection. The result is raw, revealing, and uncomfortable, but ultimately healing. I have found personal redemption.

As you read each chapter, you witnessed my transformation as I worked through the process of why I became a whistleblower. The interludes between chapters were written before, during, and after the legal process. They are a contemporaneous, chronological glimpse into the emotions I felt related to specific milestones—the beginning of retaliation, resignation from Depomed, the filing and dismissal of claims, and the settlement and moving on after litigation. During this period, the case was under seal, and I was legally bound to silence. I hope you can sense the anger, sarcasm, fear, frustration, and grief I felt during this isolation when writing was my only outlet. This book encompasses my unexpected personal and professional journey, as well as a transition from my old life to my new one.

This period of transition has been a time of reckoning and peeling off layers of anger and grief. The challenge of decluttering myself required me to move past the disappointments of litigation. One of the most liberating aspects of my post-litigation life is that I am no longer bound to legal silence. I am free to speak, share my story, and inspire others who feel the weight of institutional betrayal and corruption to come forward.

Speaking has been a path to healing and professional redemption. Publicly sharing my whistleblowing saga has given me the ability to commit to truth. It is a moral and psychological endpoint to the long and stressful legal process. The interest in my story and support of my choice to expose corruption is refreshing and humbling at the same time. The personal vindication and overwhelming encouragement from all over the world mean so much to me, especially after such a prolonged corporate and legal degradation of my spirit. In September 2025, I accepted an invitation to speak at the annual Whistleblowers of America conference on the topic of overcoming adversity, an issue faced by every whistleblower. Only two months following the resolution of the case, this was the first time I had ever spoken publicly about the ordeal, but Tully was right beside me, occasionally glancing up when my voice trembled. She stood with me as I received the Giraffe Award for "outstanding commitment to ethics, patient safety, and truth within the pharmaceutical field." Giraffe Award recipients are employees who "bravely act to improve the integrity of the agency in the face of seemingly insurmountable challenges while facing criticism and anger."

Recently, a subsequent award again humbled me. I have been selected as the 2026 recipient of the Cliff Robertson Sentinel Award by the Association of Certified Fraud Examiners (ACFE), the world's largest anti-fraud organization, for "choosing truth over self." The award is presented annually to an individual who has "bravely exposed wrongdoing in business regardless of personal or professional consequences."

To move from a decade-long silence to national and global recognition is truly a remarkable turnaround. In both cases, I am so grateful and honored to be acknowledged. These awards provide a sense of solidarity with other whistleblowers. We have all faced retaliation and betrayal and bear the deep scars of truth-telling. In accepting the awards, I also honor and recognize their sacrifices.

Whether writing or speaking, I have always had a dog by my side. From Sammy to Tully, and all of the dogs in between, they helped me find courage when I felt defeated or misunderstood, which was often. My reinvented life in the service dog world was already underway by the time the settlement came, but now I can fully dedicate myself to it. In the presence of dogs, service or otherwise, my soul is no longer conflicted. In the presence of their innate goodness, I am not pressured to lie, mislead, or feel responsible for harm. I am finally living a life that aligns with my conscience—in true service to others, not a thinly veiled corporately manufactured idea based on profit. Service and kindness to others, regardless of species, continue to heal my wounded soul.

Out of immense gratitude for Tully and all our canine companions, I feel a deep responsibility to give a voice to our longest and truest companions by sharing the beauty and science of this relationship with others. And I now have a platform to do that. One of my greatest professional joys is my role as a core faculty member at Bergin University of Canine Studies. My dog discipleship has come full circle, from student to teacher. I have the honor of teaching the undergraduate and graduate students about a dog's emotions, personality, and language, and the psychology of positive reinforcement training. Teaching others to think like a dog and feel the joy in their dog's "dogness" is exactly what I have been doing my entire life. This is a dream come true! So much of the past decade was joyless, but this is pure delight! To guide future dog handlers on how to connect with their most precious gift, as I have connected with Tully, is a gift to myself. At leashofcourage.com, I share my experience and knowledge with others about how to foster a deep connection with their own dogs. I encourage you to visit and hope to inspire a more mindful, compassionate relationship with your dog and maybe even yourself.

Taking stock and looking inward is an evolution. My journey through the past decade has been one of un-becoming what wasn't truly me and then repairing, refining, and sharpening who I am meant to be. Like the ancient Japanese art of Kintsugi, in which broken pottery is repaired with gold to strengthen and highlight the damage, my own perceived flaws are being transformed into beauty and strength. I am acknowledging the deep wounds and filling them with the golden gift of understanding. With the most exquisite, purest form of Gold by my side, I am ultimately creating a stronger and more fulfilled life, my personal Kintsugi.

Creativity is the quiet force that has the power to heal me. Writing and painting are bridges back to my truest self, offering me a path to transform pain into something beautiful. As the whistleblower ordeal shrank my world, creativity expanded it, forming an extended family I never anticipated. The Magic 8

Ball that sits on my bookshelf predicts "without a doubt" that more creativity and connection are in my future. And in the Truth or Bologna game of life, this is truth.

I'll end the saga here with another sure thing in my life: Tully, my protector and guide. We have become wiser together; our matching glasses prove it! Much to her dismay, she now shares her toys, beds, and me with two mischievous dog brothers, "The Hooligans." But Tully remains steadfast in her role as Chief Comforter. She occupies the shotgun position in my car and the most coveted place on the couch. Tully and I thank you from the bottom of our synchronized hearts for joining us on this life journey of defeat and redemption. Until we meet again, dear reader, know how much I appreciate you and welcome you into my new extended family.

Courage of My Heart

"Your vision will become clear only when you look into your own heart. Who looks outside, dreams; who looks inside, awakes."
—Carl Jung

It was a time to rise,
A time to fall back
Above all,
A path to redemption.

Forged for a decade
In the fire of corruption
I faced down
Corporate demons.

The journey led me
To the center
Of me
Where the unconscious resides.

She had been waiting
A lifetime of decades
For me to come
For recognition, refinement, renewal.

I faced the internal chaos, doubts
Now I lay down the sword.
Take off my armor and stand tall
In the courage of my heart.

(January 16, 2026, manuscript completed, spirit renewed)

Acknowledgments

My heart is full of gratitude for Goody Lindley, my writing coach, editor, mentor, and, best of all, a true friend. She came into my world overflowing with enthusiasm, confidence, and warmth, and it was contagious. She was the expert gardener who could see potential in my little plot of earth. With encouragement and insight, she tilled the soil and watered the roots, eventually helping me cultivate a beautiful sanctuary. She brought healing rain and an abundance of sunshine and nourishment to my sensitive soul, dormant and weary after a decade of abandonment. She encouraged me to dig into the dirt and find the weeds that were choking out the harvest. And then she guided me to the secret path of abundance—belief in myself. My garden is in full bloom now, and I owe it all to Goody, the master gardener, whose perception and empathy found the little girl alone in the brambles of the blackberry patch and came to sit beside me.

In loving memory of Sammy, 1964-1978

About the Author

Noelle Webb is an author, teacher, passionate speaker, and the intrepid crusader who blew the whistle on pharmaceutical corruption. She holds a master's degree from Bergin University of Canine Studies and is a certified professional dog trainer and service dog trainer. She also trains humans how to find joy in their dog's dogness while sharing her wisdom on the human–canine connection, and dog emotion, personality, and language. She makes her home in the Virginia countryside, where she occasionally wrangles a stray mule and makes friends with the local horses, cows, chickens, and dogs. With creativity in her soul and striped socks on her feet, she continues to write about life's serious and sometimes not-so-serious side. You can find her at leashofcourage.com.